THE

HIGH

ROAD

D1226187

PETE YOUNG

Figure.1

Vancouver / Berkeley

THE
HIGH ROAD

A POT GROWER'S JOURNEY
FROM THE BLACK MARKET
TO THE STOCK MARKET

Cataloguing data is available from Library and Archives Canada
ISBN 978-1-77327-068-5 (pbk.)
ISBN 978-1-77327-069-2 (ebook)
ISBN 978-1-77327-070-8 (pdf)

Design by Jessica Sullivan
Proofreading by Alison Strobel
Author photograph by Gotham Studios, London, ON

Printed and bound in Canada by Friesens
Text printed on FSC, 100% PCW paper
Distributed internationally by Publishers Group West

Figure 1 Publishing Inc.
Vancouver BC Canada
www.figure1publishing.com

To my parents, for giving me the guidance,
strength, and support to become the man I am.
And to my beautiful wife, Simone,
for supporting the man I became.

I also have to give love to all the men and women
who fought before and alongside me to free this
beautiful plant. This book is your trophy as well.

CONTENTS

PROLOGUE

ON JANUARY 23, 2018, Simone and I woke up early in the Cosmopolitan, a splashy boutique hotel with a view of downtown Toronto and, from the other side of the rooftop lounge, the lake and the islands. The night before, after a wine-soaked dinner, I'd picked out what I was going to wear: a sunflower-yellow hemp suit I'd had made for our wedding. I put it on, along with one of my favourite tie-dye T-shirts, figuring I'd make a statement—except Simone was giving me that look.

"Pete," she said. "It's dated."

I kept the pants, lost the jacket, and swapped out the tie-dye for a metallic-blue-and-gold paisley shirt I picked up on our last trip to Haight-Ashbury. Then I added my two medallions, a Grateful Dead logo and a Hindu deity named Ganesha. I was also carrying a photo of my parents and a swatch of my mom's wedding dress. Simone had a locket of her father's hair, and a pendant that'd belonged to her mother—with all four parents gone, we wanted them to somehow be there with us.

I tied up my dreadlocks, making sure to leave a few dangling, and looked over at Simone. "Better?"

She smiled, gave me a hug, and said, "I'm so proud of you."

King and Bay would never know what hit it.

WE WERE IN TORONTO to ring the opening bell at the Toronto Stock Exchange. I'm the "master grower" of Indiva, a licensed producer of medical marijuana, as well as a partner in the company. Indiva has offices in Ottawa and downtown London, Ontario, and a forty-thousand-square-foot high-tech production plant in an industrial park just off the highway in London. Indiva had started trading on the TSX a month earlier.

In the hotel lobby we met up with Indiva's top brass. Koby, the COO, also works as a business lawyer in Ottawa, while the CEO, Niel, used to run a precious metals fund for an investment firm in Boston. There's Jen, the CFO, and John, who does quality control and basically runs the facility. Finally, there's Sarah, the head of client care. Sarah and I go back decades: she was the first receptionist at the London Compassion Society and she was working the counter at Hemp Nation the second time the cops raided it; so, like me, she knows what the inside of a jail cell looks like.

As we walked down Bay Street, all I could see was black suits, shiny shoes, and worried faces. I would've thought that people on Bay Street would be tap dancing down the sidewalk with hundred-dollar bills bursting out of their briefcases, but as far as I could see, everyone looked like they were on their way to a funeral.

When we got to the stock exchange you wouldn't believe the looks we were getting at first—I thought security was going to tackle me. But then we got inside, and there was a reception with coffee and juice and non-alcoholic champagne, and people kept coming up and introducing themselves to me. It seemed like everyone but everyone wanted a picture with me, the hippie pot-growing dude. Mostly I hadn't a fucking *clue* who anyone was, just more suits and shiny shoes. I had spent decades growing weed anywhere I could, in refrigerators, closets, parks, deserted islands, all the while hiding it from parents, neighbours, cops—and all of a sudden here I was, the star of the fucking stock exchange.

I WAS STANDING there shaking hands when a guy walked up to me and introduced himself—another TSX guy—and then pulled me aside. "Pete," he said, "can I ask you something?"

Here we go, I thought, since this *always* happens to me. I smiled and said sure, and of course he whipped out his phone and showed me a picture of a pot plant he'd been trying to grow, some droopy-ass ruderalis that wasn't doing well and was never going to produce anything halfway decent even if it *did* get better. "You got spider mites. And pretty bad."

"Really?"

"You see those dots? Littered all over your leaves?"

"Oh yeah," he said. I started telling him how to treat it, only by then some other guy in a dark suit had pulled out *his* phone and was showing me photos of a wilted indica that didn't look like it was going to last the week.

I asked him about his fertilizer regimen, since it looked like maybe the plant was getting battered by the metals used in cheap fertilizer. Only he didn't have time to answer, since a woman came in and told us in a chirpy voice that we were about to begin.

IF YOU'VE NEVER BEEN to a TSX bell ringing you probably think it happens in front of the stock exchange floor. As I found out that morning, it's all done in a dark little room that's more like a film set. We filed inside. There was a woman in the studio whose job was to handle the recording of the event. It turned out she was an old high school friend of Simone's called Misty who, if you can fucking believe it, was in our wedding party. So Simone and her were chatting away, catching up, what-are-you-up-to-these-days sort of thing, when another TSX rep in a business suit stepped up.

"Can I have your attention?" she called out.

We all shut up and looked at her.

"Now there's going to be a countdown. And when we get to zero, I want you all to cheer and yell and clap your hands and wave your arms around and *really* make some noise. Do you think you can do that?" We told her we could do that, and to prove it we practiced cheering and yelling and clapping and waving and *really* making some noise.

Then we took our positions. I was in the middle, standing over a big blue plastic button—there was no actual bell, but I was told it would trigger a bell-ringing sound. Niel and Koby were on either side of me. As the three founders of Indiva, we decided we'd push the button together. It dawned on me I could be the first dreadlock to ever ring in a TSX trading session.

The countdown began. Ten, nine, eight... at zero we pressed the button and a fire-alarm-type bell rang through the room. We all cheered and yelled and clapped and waved. Confetti fell like snow from the ceiling (which doesn't happen every time, but Misty pulled some strings) and collected in my dreads and around our feet, and of course someone joked the confetti should've been rolling papers. Cameras were going off and Misty was making sure it was all being recorded and the whole time I could think of one thing and one thing only: I can't fucking *believe* my journey has brought me here.

It wasn't always like this.

NYPD
GREEN

I GREW UP IN LONG BEACH, a small town on a skinny island off the coast of Long Island, New York. Which is why in my Hemp Nation days up in Canada my nickname was NYPD—it sort of sounds like "NY Petey" if you say it quickly. My dad was the trainer for the New York Rangers, meaning he got free tickets for all kinds of shit at the Gardens, like hockey games and concerts and the circus. I remember when I was really young, like seven or eight, my parents taking me to see bands like Sha Na Na and the Bee Gees.

So in some ways I had it easy, but in other ways I didn't. As a kid my nickname was Hurricane since I couldn't keep still. I was an ADHD kid and dyslexic as hell, so school was hard. I wasn't dumb by a long shot, but reading was tough and sitting still was tougher.

Once, I was at a restaurant sitting across from my mom, and I looked down at her menu and saw the words upside down. "Mom," I blurted, "I can *read* that!" From then on, I knew it'd help my reading if I just rotated the book 180 degrees and read it upside down. One other thing helped: the teacher of my remedial reading class noticed I was reading so fast my brain wasn't keeping up to my eyes, so he encouraged me to start reading slower. I can't say it cured my dyslexia but it sure helped.

Our house was in a section of Long Beach called the Canals. There were boats and water and gulls. My parents put me in every sport they could think of, hoping it would use up all that energy: hockey, soccer, football, wrestling, lacrosse. But what I really loved was the beach—surfing, boogie boarding, chicks in bikinis. All you had to do was walk down Pacific Boulevard to where the board-walk ended and there was nothing but sand and surf, and the planes bound for JFK flew so low it was like you could reach up and touch them. Back then I even thought I might be a pro surfer someday.

My best friends in the neighbourhood were a boy named Sean and two girls named Colleen and Julie. Colleen was about two years older than me, and she hung out with friends who were older than *her*, so I started hanging out with her friends. And since they were smoking pot I started too. I'm not sure exactly what age I was, but I was pretty fucking young—my brother swears I was eleven but I could've been even younger.

It was about being a rebel. It was hearing, "hey, give some to the kid, he's cool," you know? Plus it took away that feeling I always had, like for some reason I had to race through whatever I was doing so I could get to the next thing and the next thing and the next thing after *that* and if I didn't hurry time would run out and I wouldn't have time for any of it. So that was the start of it.

Before class we'd mix up Zombies, which is when you take every type of booze you can get your hands on and put it in a water bottle or whatever. (I was known for using empty French's mustard bottles.) Then we downed them. Sometimes we took White Cross pills, which was about the stupidest thing I could do since they made your heart race and your pupils turn to pinpricks, and I was hyperactive to *begin* with. Quaaludes, mescaline, and speed were on the way, though I wasn't quite there yet. Still, I'd get high with my friends in the morning, usually in an alley beside the Police Auxiliary building. Then they'd all go to high school and I'd go to junior high, baked out of my mind, not wanting to be there, just waiting for that bell to ring. If the wind was offshore and the swell was just right you *knew* the waves at Lido Beach would be overhead, and that made being in class a thousand times worse.

When I was thirteen I failed everything. I even failed gym, which was a real achievement since I was co-captain of the lacrosse team and my coach was also my gym teacher. "Pete," I remember him saying to me, "you're hardly ever here, and when you *are* here you're not *really* here so what am I supposed to do?"

That day, on the way home, I somehow lost my report card. I told my mom and she was like, "Pete, you must think I'm stupid to fall for that excuse."

"No, no, I really did lose it, and I gotta tell you something."

"What's that?"

"I failed everything."

"Jesus, Pete, you failed every subject?"

"Every single class." Right then and there I decided to quit smoking pot for a while, just to give my brain a chance to bounce back.

I GOT MY GRADES back on track. I mean they weren't great, since I was still fighting dyslexia and ADHD, and aside from remedial classes there wasn't a lot to help kids like me back then, but I was getting by. I started spending more time with my "jock" friends and all the cute girls that followed them. One of the jocks, a guy named Rob Drake, was a huge positive influence: he was a super popular kid, built like a brick shithouse, and lived a completely clean life. He had a rule with me: I could hang with him and the rest of the popular crowd, but I couldn't be high. If he caught me he gave me a shot in the arm, and the one thing you didn't want was a kid who could squat three hundred pounds teeing off on you.

At fourteen I started at Long Beach High. It had about two thousand kids in a huge concrete building, set on stilts so it wouldn't flood during hurricanes. There were a dozen sets of stairs running up from the parking lot; the stoners all hung out in Stairway Eleven, which everyone called Stairway to Heaven. It was opposite a small pond surrounded by high grass, a good place to smoke a joint or light a bowl between classes. Since I was smoking pot again that's where I hung out, though sometimes I hung out with the jocks and the surfers, who mostly carved out their turf in the cafeteria.

After school and on weekends everyone went down to the boardwalk. I'd smoke pot with the surfers under the Lincoln Boulevard boardwalk, or smoke with the stoners under the Franklin Boulevard light. Other nights, we'd pile into a car and head to Far Rockaway, a neighbourhood in Queens that was just over the bridge from Atlantic Beach, which was at the west end of Long Beach. It was a lot different than my tidy suburban town, with low-rise tenements and chain-link fences and Spanish groceries and empty lots and houses that'd caught fire and were left with soot marks and sheets of plywood for doors and windows.

Our destination was Beach 15th, or B15 as we called it, a buried little street no more than two or three blocks long. The dealers came out after dark. All you had to do was drive up and there they'd be all over your car, kids in parkas and Air Jordans saying "What you want? What you need?" and me in the back seat, shitting myself because the place looked so dangerous. Then we'd drive back over the Atlantic Beach Bridge, a nickel or dime bag of cheap Mexican brick weed in our pockets. Or maybe, if we were lucky, it'd be a nug of something good. Either way we'd be happy and laughing. To a white kid from a suburban beach town, scoring weed in the Rockaways was a fucking *thrill*.

THAT WAS THE YEAR my mom got sick. She was diagnosed with breast cancer in 1984. After a successful mastectomy, the doctors said her survival rate was in the neighbourhood of 99 percent. She went back to daily life thinking the crisis was over, only to see the cancer come roaring back. It started in her bones and spread like fucking wildfire.

After a few years and a couple more surgeries, my dad decided to quit his job—by then he'd become equipment manager with the New York Islanders—so we could all move back to my parents' hometown of St. Thomas, Ontario, to take advantage of free health care.

St. Thomas is an auto manufacturing town surrounded by corn fields in Southwestern Ontario. A famous Barnum & Bailey elephant named Jumbo got hit by a train there in the late 1800s, so there was a statue of Jumbo in a little park down on the outskirts of town. So that's basically what St. Thomas was known for—corn, go-nowhere jobs, a dead elephant, and not a whole lot of surfing. My first year there it snowed in fucking *September*. I hated it.

It didn't help that my dad, my brother, and I had to watch as my mom wasted away. Believe me: when that happens all you can think is there must be something I can fucking *do*. Of course there wasn't. She died when I was seventeen.

BY THE TIME the final bell of grade ten rang my car was already packed, surfboard on the roof. I went back to Long Beach thinking I'd work there for the summer. I moved in with my best friend, Kevin Maher, and his mom, Marie, in the upstairs apartment of their house on East Chester Street.

Kevin's dad, Tommy, was friends with my dad, so we'd known each other since we were little. To everyone but teachers and parents, Kevin was known as Toast. Despite being a complete stoner who never lifted a fucking *finger* to keep in shape, Toast was probably the most physically fit person I'd ever met: here was a guy who could put his hands on the arms of a chair, lean forward, duck his head, and slowly push himself into a handstand.

Marie was an awesome woman, and she made a huge impact on my life when it came to finances. Toast and I both worked construction and I also worked in a surf shop, so without much time to spend money I'd just throw it all under my mattress. She was making my bed one day and saw all this cash. First she raised my rent, then she said, "Look, Pete, you've got money, you're earning money, you might as well spend a little on what you want, since tomorrow you may not be able to afford it." I've always remembered that, particularly when it comes to business, and it's always served me well.

Tommy was a cop. I remember once there was a mob hit in Long Beach; later Toast and I were out front of his house when his dad pulled up in his squad car with the supposed shooter in the back seat. That sort of thing didn't happen very often in Long Beach—John Gotti had a house across the street from our junior high, so nobody but *nobody* dared get out of line.

AT FIVE IN the morning I'd wake to the bubbling sound of Toast's bong. I mostly smoked at night and on weekends, but Toast would wake and bake every morning, then race down to the boardwalk and check for waves. If the swell was pumping, he'd run home and bang on my door, rip another bong hit, and if I got up in time we'd both race down to the beach. We had to be out of the water by 7:30 to leave for work, which rarely happened if the waves were good, so our boss had to scream at us from the boardwalk. After work we'd be back on the beach again until it got dark, then there were parties and girls. And it was in the middle of that short, hot summer that me and Toast started growing our own weed.

I DON'T EXACTLY remember why we decided to grow our own, but I can guess: growing cannabis is always about one thing and one thing only, and that's money. Even if you don't sell it, growing your own means you don't have to fucking *buy* your own pot, and that means more money in your pocket.

So. A couple of five-gallon pails. Soil dug up from the backyard. Seeds rescued from a bag of shitty brick we'd bought out on B15. Two plants, living on Toast's roof. At night we'd bring them inside, since we figured cool air was bad for them.

Toast's mom had a boyfriend who lived in Valley Stream, over near the airport, so she was hardly ever at home. When she did come home we covered the plants with a sheet in the corner of Toast's room and hoped she wouldn't notice. Of course she did anyway, so Toast told her I'd brought some tobacco seeds back from St. Thomas and that's what we were growing.

"Christ almighty," she said. "I might be dumb but I ain't stupid." Right away she told Toast's dad, but my guess is he was too busy dealing with cop shit to particularly care.

"Lookit," he told us. "It's just two fucking plants. Put them on the roof and just leave them there, they'll do better than you moving them around every day."

So that's what we did. Those two plants started to grow. The only thing we knew was that only female cannabis plants produce THC-laced flowers, the part of the plant that gets you high. You can tell a female plant by the presence of white pistils, which are the sex organs—they look like little hairs sticking out of the pre-flower, and male plants don't have them. As soon as we saw white pistils we got excited and harvested and smoked it way too soon and didn't get high and that was the end of my first garden.

I went back to St. Thomas for grade eleven. When the school year was over I came back for another summer in Long Beach with Toast. Just like the summer before, we surfed and worked construction and hung out on the boardwalk and drank beers and watched surfing videos and constantly checked the weather station. Like the summer before, I slept in Toast's mom's bedroom since she was never there.

But most importantly, we started growing weed indoors.

HINDSIGHT
IS
20-20-20

THE PROBLEM WITH our rooftop grow was the same problem *every* outdoor grower faces, whether they've got a single plant on a balcony or six hundred hectares in the middle of a forest. Sooner or later, someone's going to fucking *notice*.

In our case, someone was bound to see us carrying buckets of water onto the roof every day. That same person was then going to notice what we were growing, at which point he or she would probably do one of three things. The first was nothing, which didn't happen very often. The second was call the cops. The third—and, in my experience, the most common—was show up in the middle of the night and fucking steal it. It's one of the few guarantees of my industry: outdoor grows go missing, which is one of the reasons people move indoors. Growing indoors is discreet, if you do it right. The only people who should know about it are the people who *have* to know about it.

Also, Long Island isn't exactly California. Outdoors, we got one crop per growing season, meaning one crop per year, and if that crop failed it wasn't like we had enough warm weather to squeeze in another. Indoors was another deal altogether. You could grow year-round, so long as you could recreate the conditions cannabis likes in the great outdoors.

One afternoon that summer, Toast and I were driving home from surfing a spot we called "Malibu," since it was close to a beach bar called The Malibu, when we noticed an old refrigerator someone had thrown out. Later that night we went back and threw it in the trunk of my 1980 Grand Prix, then put it in the garage behind our apartment. We shared the garage with the old lady who lived downstairs but she never went in there, and it was already filled with all our surfing shit. Even if the plants took off and started to smell like cannabis—and female plants definitely will—it didn't matter since the garage already reeked of the fibreglass resin we used to repair dings in our boards.

We got to work. We were inspired by the old Phototron system, a shitty indoor grow box we saw advertised in the pages of *High Times* magazine. First, we lined the fridge with tinfoil. Then, we hung a small fluorescent light from the roof of the fridge. We put in a fan, and connected it to a hose leading to a window in the garage wall. We used good soil and some seeds from a bag of weed we figured had some potential. The most important step was the last one. We put a lock on the fucking thing, which didn't look weird since a lot of people had garage fridges full of beer or steaks or lobster, and they kept those locked.

We were seventeen years old and our homemade Phototron was working better than a real Phototron and we were like, "holy shit, we're growing *weed* now." We watered every day or two and gave the plants 20-20-20 fertilizer, figuring if you had to fertilize tomato plants you better do the same with pot plants. We trimmed the plants to keep them bushy, gave away the trimmings, and I'm pretty sure I collected seeds for a future grow. And this time we waited till the end of summer before we harvested. The plants were bushy and covered with fine little white hairs, and even though the yield was next to nothing it got us stoned enough that we knew our days of driving out to Rockaway were coming to an end.

By the time the summer was done, Toast was talking about a closet grow in his mother's apartment. I went back to Canada knowing there was no *way* I was going to wait till the next summer to grow some more weed.

SHORTLY AFTER I got back to St. Thomas I discovered a little panelled-off room in the basement of my dad's house. There was no door or anything, just a loose piece of panelling with a hole in it where you could stick in a large nail and pry it open. Inside was an old empty oil tank, which must've fed the furnace before the house got switched over to natural gas. Instead of paying to have the thing removed, I guess the old owners just walled it up, never thinking some kid from New York was going to come along and use it for his next grow-op.

I put a few boards on top of the drum, strung a fluorescent light from the ceiling, and potted a few seeds; I think the strain was called Northern Lights, which I'd got from a Long Island grower named Eazy E. I put the panel back in place, and added a metal shelf in front as a disguise.

It was my brother who discovered it, probably because I was stoned one day and forgot to put the panel back. So he started freaking out, saying "you idiot, you *cannot* put hot lights over an oil tank, if there's a better way to start a fire I can't even fucking think of one!" He threatened to tell my father, and since I wasn't even allowed to smoke pot in the house, never mind grow it, I dismantled the grow and chucked the plants over the back fence.

Pops found out about it anyway—the plants landed in the middle of the fucking street—but I wasn't punished because it was the year after my mom died and the whole house was messed up and Dad just didn't have the energy to get mad. The truth was, when my older brother and I were little he was always on the road with the Rangers, meaning he was new at the whole parenting thing and didn't have a clue how to deal with a rebellious seventeen-year-old with a green thumb and a taste for sativa.

What did I learn from that grow? If anything, that you don't put hot fucking lights around flammable material.

I WENT LOOKING for other options, and decided I'd risk an outdoor grow at the bottom of the ravine behind our house. I planted some seeds from a strain I called "Dog Shit."

I was worried the seedlings might not get enough water if there was a dry spell. Even if it *did* rain enough, the forest canopy was thick as shit and I couldn't see how any rain would get down to my little plants, especially since the mature trees all around them had huge thirsty rooting systems. I could water them, but it'd only be a matter of time before someone noticed me carrying pails of water to the bottom of that ravine every day, and after that you could count the hours before the grow went missing. So I came up with my first automated watering system.

I got some PVC tubing and ran it from the back of an old pool house on the edge of our property all the way down to my plants. Then I cut the top off a three-litre bottle of Faygo, a cheap-ass pop you could get at Kmart or Loblaws. I attached the bottle to the top of the tubing so it worked like a funnel. Then I took a regular two-litre soda bottle and filled it with a mixture of water and Miracle-Gro and stuck it in the funnel, where it'd drip out slowly, run down the tubing, and water my plants.

I'm meticulous and hard-working as hell (maybe because I'm a Virgo). I started playing around with water-absorbing polymers, which I'd read about in a pot-growing manual from 1975 called *Growing Extraordinary Marijuana*, one of the earliest books on growing weed. Basically, a water polymer is a grainy substance that'll suck up fifty times its own weight in moisture. They're used in diapers and those toys that grow in water and all sorts of things, and they're fucking *perfect* for outdoor grows because they attract moisture away from all the competing plant life. So after rigging up my water system I mixed a bunch of polymer crystals into the soil around my plants and presto, I had a system.

Every couple weeks I'd sneak down to the ravine and check on my plants, and every time I'd smell the killer aroma and be like "holy shit, these things are fucking *growing*." Still, I was new to the game and I broke the cardinal rule: don't show people. I showed people. Not a lot, just a couple of close friends who already knew I was a grower, but that was too many. When you're growing pot you only tell people you absolutely *have* to tell. Say you need an electrician to help you steal some hydro: he gets to see it because you can't not show him. Or you have investors who want to know how their weed is doing: they get to see it since the weed is partly theirs and they likely know the cardinal rule as well as you do. If some guy gave you the seeds, some exotic fucking strain that's impossible to get: yeah, he gets to see the weed. But no one else. Not your friends, not your family, not your girlfriend. The bottom line is, it doesn't matter how much you trust people, once you start showing your plants, word *will* get around.

One day, later that fall, I went down to visit my almost mature plants and every last one of them was gone. I saw red. You know what they say: never piss off a hippie. All that suppressed rage comes to the surface.

Luckily the ravine floor was damp that day and the thieves left pretty good footprints. So I took a piece of paper and sketched the sole pattern, making sure my drawing was the exact same size. I took the drawing to a buddy of mine who worked in a shoe store, and he told me the tread belonged to a pair of Vans skate shoes. Just then, something twigged: a couple of days earlier, my brother told me he'd seen a friend of his named Devon heading toward the ravine with another guy named John. Now the hunt was really on: since I knew Devon didn't wear Vans, I figured his friend was the culprit. I found Devon at his apartment in London, and asked him, "Does that asshole buddy of yours wear fucking Vans?"

"I think he does."

I looked at him, all serious. "Devon," I finally said. "Are we really gonna go down this road?"

He paused for a moment. "Alright, alright," he said. "Let me call him."

Within an hour or so he called me back and said John still had most of it, so the next day I went back to Devon's house and I'm pretty sure I became the first grower in the history of the world to get his stolen weed back.

SEED
MONEY

THE DAY AFTER I finished high school in 1990, I returned to Long Beach to live with Toast. True to his word, he really *had* installed a garden in his bedroom closet, with a dozen or so cuttings in four-inch Rockwool cubes sitting in plastic bowls.

A surfer buddy named Rennie kept telling Toast he should switch to high-intensity discharge lamps, which produce a spectrum plants really like. We'd also heard there's something about HID light that makes it travel differently: it bends and curls, more like sunlight, so it penetrates your plant canopy better and gets to the leaves on the bottom. HID lamps can even be cheaper than regular fluorescent tubing. We made a deal: if Ren supplied the lights, he'd get part of the harvest.

We couldn't believe the fucking difference it made: our very next crop came up with actual nugs on the plants, instead of a few wispy flowers. Instantly, we were HID enthusiasts. We soon learned there are different kinds of HID lamps—metal halides have a cool blue glow that's perfect for the vegetative phase, and high-pressure sodium HIDs are more of an orange-red colour that helps the plants flower—so we started changing the type of HID lamps according to the plant's growing cycle.

We also learned a crucial fact about soil, which is that you don't even fucking *need* it. Rockwool is a fibre made from basalt and chalk; the fibre is pressed into cubes, which you then stick your seeds into. It was originally used for insulation, but then some smart guy in Denmark started growing roses in it, the advantage being that Rockwool holds a perfect ratio of moisture and air. We were now in the world of HID lighting and hydroponics.

We were also getting interested in genetics. We traded for seeds from all over, especially if we heard some surfer buddy was going to California or Mexico. Genetics soon became my special interest, mostly since Toast wasn't much into it at first. It was perfect for me, though. I'm analytical as *fuck* (a Virgo, remember)—I've still got a collection of almost every strain I've ever grown, hundreds of different varieties, all labelled and stored in jars or little baggies.

We worked construction, surfed whenever we could, and grew pot. Our plants were coming up nicely, some short and bushy, others tall and lanky, some in the middle. Sativa versus indica, in other words.

When it comes to cannabis—and plants in general—geography tells you a lot about the plant. Sativas come from hot places closer to the equator, like Mexico or

Jamaica, where they grow tall and airy to keep themselves cool. Indicas are short and clustered, since they come from the mountainous areas of Afghanistan, where it's cold at night, so the plant does everything in its power to stay warm. Since sativas can grow all year round, they're in no hurry to flower, and can take up to sixteen weeks to mature. Indicas, on the other hand, come from places with seasons, and since they're in a hurry to flower they can take as little as seven or eight weeks. The yields are different, too: a sativa grown under a 1,000-watt bulb might only net you about a half-pound of pot, whereas an indica might get you one or two pounds plus.

It's no wonder the large-scale grow market is so intensely focused on indica, since it grows faster and yields more. Plus, the sativa plants can get fucking big: if they're happy, they can grow to fifteen feet, *easy*, meaning if you're trying to grow them indoors you're spending all your time pruning and training the thing to fit the size of your room. On top of all *that*, with Bush's War on Drugs in full effect at the time, the various drug enforcement agencies were cracking down on marijuana importation, with the courts handing out fucking life sentences in Texas if you got caught with a few joints in your luggage. Naturally, this didn't reduce the amount of pot on the street, it just meant that crossing borders was riskier, so the pot on the street started coming from domestic gardens. Again, this favored indica: it naturally grows better in cooler, shorter, seasonal climates, which meant that the whole North American market was turning to indica, indica, and more indica.

Which was a shame if you preferred smoking sativa. I always say the difference between sativa and indica is getting high and getting stoned. Sativa gets you high: think of a Mexican farmer, working in the field and smoking all day, using the plant for a bit of motivation. Indica knocks you on your ass: picture some guy in Afghanistan lying around in a hash house, puffing on a hookah filled with Hindu Kush, nothing to do but stare at the ceiling.

Back when I still smoked pot I was always a sativa guy, since I liked to get things fucking *done*. I'd pick bricked-up Mexican sativa over the finest commercial indica. The only thing I didn't like about classic hot-climate sativa was the taste: down in Mexico or the Caribbean, they cured it by just leaving it out in the sun, which burns off all the terpenes that give cannabis its beautiful aromas. That's why brick weed always tasted like burnt pigeon ass, whereas indica tasted like lavender or blueberries or pine.

After a while, domestic growers realized they were missing out on a huge market by only growing indica. This is when hybrids came in—plants that grew like indica but had the psychoactive effect of sativa. In the late '90s, I came up with a short, bushy, fast-growing hybrid that I called Golden Haze, which both growers and smokers loved; I sold a shitload of those seeds. I also came up with an indica that did well outside, which I called "New York Skunk, New York Skunk," the strain so nice we named it twice. I couldn't sell enough of it, and I wasn't alone. Growers all started looking for that perfect balance: it's what modern-day connoisseurship is all about. Today, there are literally thousands of genetic hybrids out there, sativa-indica blends that grow like indica and act like sativa, or vice versa, and keep both growers and smokers happy.

That closet grow with Toast was my first real success, in that it produced a good amount of pot that got you high and tasted pretty good. We split the harvest three ways: a third to Toast, since the grow was in his closet; a third to Rennie, for his help with the lighting; and a third to a friend of Rennie's, a surfer named Pete, who gave us some seeds. Then they each pieced off a decent portion for me, which I mostly shared with friends or family.

I was never really in the game to sell weed to the recreational market—that's how you find yourself surrounded by some pretty sketchy people. And I've always believed the plants sense when they're being grown for profit, and they don't fucking like it. So even back then, I considered myself a *grower*, full stop.

This was our life. We grew pot, we surfed, we worked. After a day of swinging a hammer we'd smoke weed and watch the weather channel, or surfing videos, and eat lobster (a lot of our surfer buddies worked at the local lobster farm). The days passed in a blur.

GROWING UP, I'd always thought I'd become a professional surfer. I entered a few competitions and did well enough, but my surfing career came to a crashing fucking halt when my family moved to Ontario. I was pretty miserable, so to make it up to me my parents bought me a gorgeous camera, the Minolta Maxxum 5000. With all the lenses it probably cost over $1,000 (today you can buy a used one on Craigslist for fifteen bucks).

I loved it. The first thing I did was spend all afternoon taking pictures of squirrels in the backyard. When I went back to Long Beach in the summers, I started taking photos of two things. The first was surfers, since there was a real culture of surf photography and I figured I could stay close to the sport that way. My other subject was cannabis. I photographed all the plants Toast and I grew, documenting them in every stage, and if I heard about a nice grow someone else had I'd ask to shoot it, too.

After a year back in Long Beach I decided to apply to the photography program at Fanshawe College in London, Ontario, just a little north of my dad's place in St. Thomas. My grades were pretty shitty so I was put on a waiting list. Four days before classes started, Fanshawe called and told me I was in. I boogied back up to Canada and started going to classes while living with my dad, travelling back and forth in his Nissan pickup.

At the end of the year, the class held a photo competition for first-year students. They only let you show black and white (something to do with learning the basics), and one of the best black-and-white photos I'd ever taken was of that fridge grow Toast and I had years earlier. So I figured fuck it, I'll submit it. The other students displayed photos of buildings and flowers and people and the sort of shit people usually take pictures of, and there was my shot, on display for all my classmates and teachers to see—a top view of a gorgeous sticky nug I'd hand-coloured so the image would really pop. I got noticed. Cannabis photography is a big thing now, but back then you hardly ever saw it unless you read *High Times*, which not a whole lot of people did.

As it turned out, there was some other guy in my class who'd been taking pictures of nugs, and he was trying to sell them at a new shop downtown called The Great Canadian Hemporium.

THE HEMPORIUM WAS small, maybe four hundred square feet, but it sold stuff I'd never seen in a store before, like pipes, screens, grow guides. A lot of the bongs were made by an Arizona-based company called Graffix; though the market is crowded now, back then Graffix was the only mass-producer of cannabis smoking devices. The Hemporium mostly focused on locally produced, cannabis-themed artwork, like paintings and wood carvings and homemade tie-dye.

I was looking around one day when a guy came out of the back. He looked about fourteen years old, with some newly formed blonde dreads and little round glasses. I asked him if he'd be willing to sell my photos of pot on consignment.

"Sure," he said, and that's how I met Chris Clay.

FREE
MARIJUANA

CHRIS AND I WERE BOTH into photography and weed and we were more or less the same age, but in other ways, we were complete opposites; Chris was from London, Ontario, and was careful and quiet and clean-cut, and I was this hippie New York surfing dude, fast talking and long-haired and quick with an opinion. Yet in our own ways we were both headstrong and determined, and maybe that's why we clicked.

Chris studied photography at Ryerson University in Toronto. At the time, Ryerson had a program that let you do an entire year of classes during a summer on Prince Edward Island. Chris went. While he was there, one of the other students had a buddy back home FedEx him a bunch of pot. Chris, who was nineteen years old and had never smoked a joint in his *life*, was all worried since he'd listened to all that bullshit they taught you in health class, how weed kills your brain cells and gives your children birth defects and turns you into a fucking axe-murderer. But he tried some anyway and liked it.

When Chris got back to Toronto he went to the school library and researched the fuck out of cannabis. The more peer-reviewed studies on the health implications of marijuana use he read the more he came to two conclusions: weed is less of a health risk than alcohol or tobacco, and Canada's marijuana laws were unfair. So he went into business.

Chris has an entrepreneurial streak a mile wide (so do I; maybe that's another reason we got along). He started selling pipes, bongs, grow guides, and hemp products, mainly through appearances at events like Lollapalooza and Hempfest, an annual cannabis conference promoting decriminalization. He made a *shit*load of money from both, so he started selling at a weekly flea market in London, and by the spring of 1992, he'd rented a space in a crappy run-down mall.

To promote his new storefront he placed an ad in the *London Free Press*, the big establishment newspaper in London, that read in part:

FREE MARIJUANA

Information

He was flooded with customers. But some readers complained that the *Free Press* was promoting drug use, so the paper refused to run the ad again. Chris sent a press release to all the major news outlets, complaining that the *Free Press* had suppressed his right to free speech. *Global News* took the bait and ran a piece on Chris's store, which gave him so much publicity he couldn't keep up with demand.

Shortly after that he applied for a "Youth Venture Loan" with the Royal Bank. When the bank rep showed up, Chris told her he wanted the money to expand his operation. She looked around, stony-faced, and finally said, "I don't agree with your store, but I can see you're going to make a go of it." She gave him $7,500.

I don't think she knew that selling marijuana paraphernalia was illegal. But Chris did.

IN 1988, the Ontario government banned sales of pot paraphernalia in an attempt to shut down all the seedy head shops along Yonge Street in Toronto. This was one of the main reasons Chris opened the store—in his mind, The Great Canadian Hemporium would be a direct challenge to laws he saw as unjust and hypocritical.

At first it didn't work, at least not by Chris's strange definition of success. Yes, he was making a lot of money. The only problem was the cops didn't seem to give a shit. So, shortly after I met him, he decided to push the envelope a little further by selling seeds. Not sterilized hemp seeds, which people use as a non-psychoactive ingredient in cooking—he'd been selling those since the flea market days. He wanted to sell real, germinating seeds that you could plant and grow.

This is where I came in. At the time, Chris already had a basement grow with a few friends in the house he was renting on Elmwood, a suburban street full of large, modern homes. The place was always full of hippies coming and going. I was never quite sure who lived there and who was just popping by. I liked it: it was laid back and fun and had a real Haight-Ashbury vibe. But, as smart and business savvy as Chris was, it was obvious he knew jack shit about growing.

Shortly after I showed up, a light came away from the ceiling and landed in a plant and burnt the fucking thing to death. I also noticed his ballasts were all wrong—ballasts are a sort of transformer you need to run HID lamps, and there are different types for different stages of a plant's life. So if a falling light didn't cause a fire then a wiring malfunction would. Plus the place was dirty and there were cuttings everywhere and the number one rule is if you want your plants to do well you have to show them some fucking *respect*. This one natty-dreaded white guy was growing pot in a basement sink full of dirt, with the tap for a water source. I was like, "are you fucking *kidding* me?"

So I helped him out. Luckily, I knew what the hell I was doing. I fixed the lighting and, using some of Chris's money, bought better equipment and started growing out some of the strains I'd been collecting over the years. Then I got to work.

To grow a good seed stock, you start by getting a bunch of seeds that, with any luck, are from plants similar to the plants you want to grow. Then you grow them out, at which point you're going to notice something: some of the plants will be healthy and bushy, some will look sickly as shit, and some will be somewhere in the middle. If you're familiar with your parent seeds, you're also going to notice that some look like the mother plant and some look like the father plant.

This is called your first generation, or your F1. (You'd think it would be G1, but the F stands for filial.) Now, you take a whole bunch of cuttings from the best females in the batch, and just one or two cuttings from the best males. Why? It only takes one or two male plants to pollinate a room full of females: you can literally shake a male plant over the females and watch the pollen fall off. Or, you can shake a male plant in front of a fan and dose the entire room that way.

Now, you grow out a second batch using those cuttings. Again, some of the plants'll be awesome and some not so much, but the difference between the good and bad plants won't be as noticeable, and the average plant in your F2 crop will be a hell of a lot healthier than your average plant in your F1 crop. So you repeat. You do it all again. By your third generation—your F3—all of your plants should look similar to your first generation mother and father plant. If they don't, you do it one more time and I guarantee each female will produce hundreds of super high-quality seeds.

For Chris's store, I created a mind-warping mixture of a Skunk No. 1 seed I'd picked up in New York, and my old favourite, Northern Lights, both of them potent sativa-indica blends from the states. It even had a nice nutty flavour, if I do say so myself. Pretty soon, word got out that The Great Canadian Hemporium was selling high potency, third- and fourth-generation seeds; if I remember right, we sold ten seeds for twenty-five dollars. To make kick-ass weed out of them, buyers just had to grow them out.

The trick is to remove all of the male plants as soon as the plants reveal their sex. If you do this, the female plant will get as desperate as a cat in heat. Her calyx, that little red tongue protruding from the pistil, will produce a rich resin that attracts male pollen. And if that pollen isn't around, the female plant will produce more and more resin—and it's this resin that's full of THC, the active ingredient in marijuana. An unfertilized female plant will grow up without producing seeds. The result is sinsemilla—or "without seed" in Spanish—which is commonly, and mistakenly, referred to as a strain of pot. It isn't: it's weed that's been made more potent by not letting the female plant pollinate.

CHRIS'S SEED BANK got bigger and bigger, just to keep up with demand. We grew nonstop in the basement of his house, and rented apartments and houses throughout London to use as grow houses (all while I was studying full-time at Fanshawe). Still, the cops didn't seem to care. Chris even put a seed menu of our different strains and hybrids, complete with prices, in the shop window.

He'd watch the cops stop to read it—and then just laugh and move on.

We couldn't believe it. We were new to the game, and we didn't yet understand who gets busted for pot and who doesn't. Here's the way I saw it: 90 percent of those who get into the growing and selling of marijuana stand a pretty good chance of getting caught. A neighbour notices people coming and going at all hours, or the hydro company gets wise, or someone catches a whiff. Pretty soon, someone is going to phone the cops and then the cops pretty much have to do something.

About 10 percent, however, never get arrested. Roughly half of those are aging hippies or introverts who live way out in the woods and don't take any chances. They don't buy supplies in the same town where they live, and when they do buy supplies, they rent a car so nobody learns what their truck looks like. The other half are people like Chris and myself, people who're operating right under the noses of the cops.

Now if you're a cop, the chances are you don't want the headache. You just *know* the guy's going to fight the charge, if only to make a statement about some goddamn thing, meaning you're going to spend all your time in court, which is boring as shit and costly to the department since now they need to find someone to do your job while you're waiting around in court. It's even worse if the so-called criminal is a fresh-faced kid with glasses named Chris Clay, who you just *know* will get a ton of sympathy when the media gets ahold of the story.

So you look the other way. You hope no one complains, so you can just let it go.

By this point, Chris had already contracted a lawyer, an Osgoode Hall law prof named Alan Young. In addition to being pro-marijuana, Young provided legal services to people whose real crime was having an alternative lifestyle. In London, he was best known for defending a local bookstore owner who'd been hit with obscenity charges for selling a

2 Live Crew album that was banned in Ontario. (His name was Marc Emery, the same Marc who later became known as Canada's "Prince of Pot.") Later, Young fought for a woman's right to go topless in public in Ontario, and he defended a dominatrix named Terri-Jean Bedford who'd been arrested on prostitution charges. Young was also the director of the Innocence Project, in which he taught Osgoode Hall law students how to fight cases of wrongful conviction and imprisonment.

He was the perfect lawyer for Chris. The two of them quickly cooked up a plan: when Chris finally managed to get himself arrested, Young would defend him by launching a constitutional challenge to Canada's marijuana laws.

But no matter what he did, Chris couldn't get arrested. He even took out ads in local papers to promote his seed bank, promising to "Overgrow the Government," and he *still* couldn't get a rise out of the police.

I FINISHED MY YEAR at Fanshawe College and went back to Long Beach to surf, work construction, and start handing out my resume in New York City. I couldn't live with Toast (his mom had broken up with her boyfriend and moved back in to her bedroom full-time), so I moved in with a friend of Toast's named Paul Levesque, whose mom rented me a small bachelor apartment in her basement at a preferred rate. Paul had a two-light closet grow, so we started experimenting with different clones.

Being friendly with the weed dealers on Long Island came in handy; if they got ahold of something interesting, they'd pass a few seeds my way. One of these was a huge pot dealer named Joe, whose dad happened to be the guy Toast's mom had been dating. Another was a guy named Ian, who passed on a really interesting sativa-indica hybrid we started calling Big E. Bud.

I started helping other people with their gardens around this time, something I've done ever since. Again, it was a karma thing: somehow your own plants know if you're spreading goodwill, and will do better. I know that sounds granola as shit but it's true. Plants are living entities and somehow they *know*.

There was another benefit. Every time I helped someone with a garden, I'd ask if I could have a few seeds, which I'd jar and label and include a few notes about its growing characteristics and pharmaceutical effects. I soon became known as the seed guy, so if someone had some interesting weed they'd smuggled back from someplace like California or Mexico or maybe even Asia, they'd give me a few seeds.

ONE TIME I HELPED a friend of a friend of a friend, an older guy named Ron with a big handlebar moustache, who was growing a sativa-dominant hybrid in his backyard. What Ron didn't realize is that nothing grows faster, or bigger, than a happy sativa. This one must've been fucking ecstatic: the thing had to have been a dozen feet high. Worse, the plant was still juvenile, so Ron couldn't even harvest it yet. He was completely freaking out, saying, "Pete, Pete, the thing's growing a few inches a day, someone's going to see it and steal it, or the cops'll bust me, Jesus, Pete, what the *fuck* should I do?"

I told him to calm down and we got to work. First, I showed him how to train the thing sideways and trellis it so at least it'd be hidden by the fence. Then, I showed him how to *keep* it growing horizontally instead of vertically. It was either that, I told him, or cut the thing down and chalk it up to experience. Naturally he wouldn't do that—you can easily get a pound of nugs off a plant that size—so he thanked me and we smoked a little pot and then I left.

A couple of nights later, someone started hammering on the door of my apartment. I answered and there was Ron, gripping a baseball bat and saying, "gimme my fuckin' plant back."

I knew instantly what must've happened. Despite our efforts, someone had noticed his massive sativa and come in the middle of the night and dug the thing up, and now he was working his way down the list of people who'd seen his overgrown plant. It was nothing personal; it's just what you do. I'd have done the same.

"Come on in," I said. He came in. "Have a seat," I said. He sat down on my little single bed. "Listen. Would I have really put in all that work if I was just going to come back in the middle of the night and destroy it? Plus, the plant wasn't even flowering yet so only a complete amateur would've stolen it. Do I *look* like a complete fucking amateur?"

He thought for a moment. "Yeah, you're right," he said. "But you just gotta try everyone, you know?"

"I get it," I told him, and that was that.

POT SEEDS
IN MY
FANNY PACK

I WENT BACK TO Ontario in early September to do my last year at Fanshawe. I was broke as shit, so I applied to the Ontario Student Assistance Program. They gave me $4,500, half of it a grant and half of it a loan. I went out and bought a pound of magic mushrooms.

After picking up some scales, I carefully divvied up the shrooms into quarter-ounce bags, making sure I had exactly the same amount of caps, stems, and dust in each bag. I remember doing it in the bathroom of my girlfriend's house, since my dad was home and I didn't want him to know what I was up to. Her name was Angela. I don't think she ever knew exactly what I was doing in there. I sold it slowly, only to friends and classmates, and by the time I finished I'd tripled my investment. I used the money to buy my school supplies, which cost a lot when you're in the photography program.

I had a classmate who was a rock photographer from Sarnia named Richard. He was a few years older than me and had already followed the Dead around on a few tours. He'd smuggle cameras into the shows, take photos of the band, and then sell them in the parking lot of the next show, making enough money to get from one show to the next, and the next, and the next. He also had a tie-dye company called Limited Edition, and he sold his own T-shirts at shows.

One day when he and I were talking he mentioned he went to Europe every year to shoot rock concerts. I asked if I could tag along and he said sure. He went over in March 1993, and a week later I joined up with him. We were just two guys and a station wagon filled with photography equipment. We went to Holland, Belgium, France, and Spain, mostly camping in the car. To take bags of weed over borders, we'd stuff them in mayonnaise jars or wheel wells. By the time we got to Amsterdam, Richard had to go to London, something to do with a girlfriend who was pissed at him for something I can't quite remember. Maybe it was because he was smoking his way around Europe with me and not her.

So I was alone in Amsterdam for a couple of days. At every café I bought pot, carefully packaged and labelled any seeds, and asked other travellers at the hostels to roll joints for me—which sounds weird, I know, since I'd been smoking pot since I was eleven (or was it ten?) and had been growing since I was fifteen. But I always smoked with bongs, and so did all my friends. (Everyone's vaping these days, but if you're still using a bong, here's a little advice: use warm water. It might not cool the throat as much but it removes way more tar.)

I wandered around with my pockets full of joints and a tall can of Heineken in my hand. I got tired of the tourist zones real quick, so I'd take long, long walks, wandering into bars and weed cafés that'd never seen a tourist, sometimes getting totally fucking lost and then feeling a little of that indica anxiety if I couldn't find my way back. But then I found I was having a lot more fun when I had no idea where I was. Once, I gave up trying to find my hostel and crawled under a boat beside a canal, only to be woken up by some drunk guy pissing on it.

Along the way, I discovered something interesting. Everyone had told me I'd be blown away by Dutch pot, but I wasn't. At all. The stuff tasted terrible. It was potent enough, but it didn't hold a candle to the genome-selected sinsemilla I was growing in chilly old London, Ontario. And unless I mixed the weed with tobacco, which I hate doing, my joints kept going out—a sure sign there was still fertilizer in the cannabis flowers.

During the last two weeks of a grow you have to switch from fertilized water to plain water to flush out all the salt and fertilizer that's absorbed into a plant. The Dutch were growing their cannabis in the same way they grew their fucking tulips, meaning they fertilized right to the end of the growth cycle. When I smoked the weed in Holland, the ash was hard and black, which told they weren't flushing. Plus, like I said, the stuff tasted like burnt hair.

I FLEW BACK to Ontario, pot seeds hidden in my fanny pack, having tasted what life could be like if marijuana was legal in Canada. Back in London, the cops were still turning a blind eye to Chris Clay's illegal seed bank. Jean Chrétien was promising to either legalize or decriminalize, and none of the opposition parties seemed to have a problem with that. I felt like Canada's marijuana laws were bound to change soon.

A few weeks after that, Chris finally got busted.

He had placed an ad in the *London Free Times* advertising Skunk No. 1 cuttings for twenty-five bucks apiece. The day the ad came out, he sold cuttings to exactly six customers. The first five wanted to grow pot. The sixth was an undercover drug squad officer, who came back shortly afterward and busted Chris. The narc also busted the guy who actually sold him the cutting, a Hemporium employee named Jordan Prentice. (You might recognize Jordan; he was born with dwarfism, and is an actor best known for starring in the film *In Bruges* with Colin Farrell and Ralph Fiennes.) It was a Friday afternoon. The cops took Chris and Jordan down to the station, then packed up everything in the store and confiscated it.

As soon as I heard Chris got busted, I knew it was only a matter of time before they searched his house on Elmwood. So I raced over there and, with the help a friend of ours called Prozac—his real name was Zack—and his girlfriend and a few others, pulled apart Chris's basement grow. Sure enough, the cops showed up about an hour later. There were still lights hanging from the ceiling and a thick trail of dirt leading up the steps, out the back door, and right to the fence that separated the backyard from an open field. In that field, right against the fence, was a mound of ripped-up pot plants.

When the cops asked if any of us knew anything about it, we were all like, "Officer, we don't know how that got there, kids're always partying in that field so maybe that's how..." The police detained Prozac and his girlfriend, though they never charged them and soon let them go.

They still charged Chris with trafficking and possession and a bunch of bullshit paraphernalia charges. (They charged Jordan with the same offences, more or less, though the charges were later dropped.) They kept Chris alone in a cell throughout the weekend, and let him out on $5,000 bail on Monday morning. He immediately contacted Alan Young, his lawyer in Toronto. The game was on.

THERE ARE A few ways to fight a criminal charge. One is to plead guilty and hope they give you a light sentence for not wasting the court's time with a trial. The second is to plead not guilty and try to prove you didn't do it. A third is to say "yeah, I did it all right, but I'm not guilty because the law I broke is horseshit and here's why"—that's basically what a constitutional challenge is.

Chris had been waiting to launch his challenge since the day he first opened the Hemporium, so he was excited and optimistic. Instead of keeping a low profile, he moved out of his tiny store in the mall, went into debt to expand the inventory, and opened a much larger place on Richmond Street in downtown London. He changed the name of the store to Hemp Nation, which he felt better reflected the outfit's new militancy.

Soon, a regular crew took shape: we called ourselves the Hemp Nation family. There was Chris of course, who everyone called HB, for Hemp Boy. I was NYPD or just NY. A guy we called Wild Willy managed the store; later we started calling him the Minister of Labour. There was a feisty artist named Andrew, the Minister of Defence. And there were a bunch of other part-time employees, volunteers, friends and sympathizers: Ben, Skip, OG, Picky Head, Sandra, G Boogie, Sarah. I started carrying a pager in case any of us got in trouble.

I started working in the store on weekends in addition to running the seed portion of the business. I also ran "How to Grow" seminars at the store on Sunday afternoons, using tomato plants instead of pot plants so I could keep my ass out of jail. For this, I became the Minister of Agriculture. At the time I was the only one with a vehicle, a white Nissan pickup truck my dad gave me. I named it Cool Runnings, after the Bob Marley song, and put a pot leaf decal in the back window.

One day, I was driving downtown and I looked out and I saw Zack sprinting down the street, which was weird since you never, ever saw him on foot. The store had a communal bicycle called the Cannabis Cruiser and Zack used it all the time. When I saw him running flat out, his dreads flying behind him, I fucking *knew* my pager was gonna go off.

Sure enough it did. I called the store and Chris told me the cops were on their way to Prozac's new apartment. So I headed downtown and picked up Chris and headed to Prozac's, where he was pacing in little circles, hyper-ventilating, and looking worried as shit. In between breaths he explained what'd happened.

He'd heard a knock and opened the door to see a seriously pissed-off looking middle-aged guy. "Who the hell are you?" the guy said.

"I live here," Zack answered. "I'm subletting from some friends." This was true; he had a met a couple university girls through the store.

"Well I haven't got a cent from those girls in months."

The landlord demanded to be let into the apartment to take a look around. Zack protested, saying, "Hey, wait a fucking *minute*, you can't just come in like this."

"Lookit," said the landlord, "either you let me take a look around my property, or I'll just come back with the cops."

So Zack let him in, explaining his girlfriend was asleep in the bedroom and he shouldn't disturb her. The landlord just said "Open the fucking door." Zack did, and the landlord found about four hundred infantile clones on a grow table.

"So," he said to Zack. "I'm going now, and I'm coming back with the cops, and if all that pot is still there when we get back, you're going to jail."

The guy left. Zack ran to Hemp Nation to make a call and *that's* when I'd seen him running flat out down the street.

I parked the truck in the lane at the back and we carried tray after tray of clones out of his apartment, which just happened to be at Oxford and Richmond, one of the busiest intersections in downtown London. We pulled out grow tables and HID lighting systems and aluminum shades and bags of fertilizer and then—after all *that*—the cops never even fucking showed up. It was all just a ruse to force Prozac to get the weed out of his apartment.

IT TURNED OUT that launching a constitutional challenge was slow and expensive. Even though Chris's lawyers, Alan Young and an associate named Paul Burstein, were working pro bono, it would take a lot of money to secure expert witnesses and evidence: about $200,000, according to Young.

Chris was already in debt from opening his new, bigger store, so the first thing he did was move back in with his parents to reduce his overhead. He then designed a Hemp Nation website and started asking for donations online. Money started rolling in. The internet was brand new back then; there weren't a whole lot of websites asking for money to help overthrow Canadian drug laws. The average donation was pretty low, like ten or fifteen bucks, but there were a lot of them. Weirdly, a fair bit of the money came from outside of Canada. I guess stoners like to stick together no matter what country they come from.

In the basement of the new store, Chris found an old sign advertising Victory Bonds, which gave him an idea: he printed up his own Victory Bonds and sold them for twenty-five dollars. Buyers were promised a quarter-ounce of pot on the day that marijuana possession became legal in Canada. All the money raised was dedicated to the constitutional challenge.

At Hemp Nation, business was booming thanks to all the free publicity from media coverage of the arrest. We were selling everything we'd sold before the raid—pipes, bongs, books, hemp clothing—with the exception of cuttings. Among our biggest sellers were my seeds, which Chris started hawking online as a mail-order product. With these three revenue streams—the website, the Victory Bonds, and the store—Chris quickly raised enough money to get himself out of debt and get his lawyers working away on his challenge.

There was only one problem. We were running out of fucking seeds, largely because we'd lost both Chris's and Zack's gardens. As Minister of Agriculture, this became my problem. To solve it, I rented an apartment on William Street, just on the outskirts of downtown. I put a 400-watt HID lamp in a closet to grow cuttings, and in a bedroom I strung 1,000-watt lights to grow the plants out. Chris helped out with the rent and grow equipment.

This time, I went with what's called an ebb and flow, which is a hydroponic system that, through the use of a mushroom valve, senses when water levels are low and refills itself. It was also my first time using the trellis method for my own garden; I methodically cut all the plants so they spread horizontally instead of vertically. This way they would all be the same height and get the same amount of light. I grew indica or indica-based strains: my usual workhorses of Skunk No. 1 and Northern Lights, as well as Golden Boy, Bubble Gum, DMB, Big Bud, Soma, and others. It was my most sophisticated set-up so far.

My girlfriend at the time, Tara, also lived with me. She was a fairly straitlaced girl who worked in the service industry. When we first met there was no real connection, but one night she decided she needed to see me, so she climbed into my place through the back window, somehow breaking her ankle on the way in, and I came home to find her passed out drunk on my bed. I took her to the hospital in the morning and we bonded in the waiting room. She moved in shortly after and we were together the next two and a half years.

Here's my point: even though Tara was living with me, I saw no reason why she needed to know about the garden I had in the locked second bedroom. Instead, I told her the room belonged to my roommate, Danny, who was away travelling in Europe. In reality, "Danny" was a reference to a strain I was growing in that room that'd been pioneered by another London grower named Dan Miller, who had a garden in an apartment above Hemp Nation. He was growing a powerful indica up there that everyone fucking loved, but he wasn't sure what strain it was so we all started calling it "Dan Miller's Bud" or just DMB. So when I told her that "Danny" lived in the locked bedroom, I wasn't totally lying (or at least that's the way I saw it).

After a while I felt a little ridiculous always making up shit about my travelling roommate. One day Tara was on the sofa reading a book when she looked over at me and asked if I had any idea when Danny was thinking of coming back.

"You know," I told her, "I think it's time you met my roommate."

She followed me to the room. I unlocked and opened the door. Tara looked in at a room so full of nearly mature female cannabis plants that it looked like a fucking jungle.

"Huh," she said. "I figured it was something like that."

Then she went back to her reading.

WITH MY NEW ebb and flow system I started seeing better results than I'd ever had before. My very first harvest yielded one and three-quarter pounds of high-grade sinsemilla, an astounding amount of pot for a single light.

Of course, there were problems. Shortly after I set up the garden, my neighbour complained about a hum coming from my apartment. It was from a 1,000-watt ballast I'd hung on the wall we shared. "Oh yeah," I told him, "the fridge is old as hell, I'd been meaning to talk to the landlord about that. Don't worry, I'll get right on it." I moved the ballast to another wall. Then, in case the neighbour on the other side heard the hum, I found a crappy air-conditioner unit that didn't even work and stuck it in the window. I even rigged up a little drip system and connected it to a five-gallon pail, so if the neighbour looked at it he'd think it was just an old dripping air-conditioner and no wonder it was so fucking loud.

To complete the set-up I built what I call a "Bounce box," an invention I still recommend to indoor growers. Cannabis doesn't do well if the air it's breathing is too warm or still or humid, so I was pulling nice cool air from the crawlspace between floors and blowing it over the plants. Before exhausting this air out the side of the house, I ran it through a one-foot square by three-feet deep wooden box filled with Bounce fabric softener sheets. This disguised the cannabis smell, though my neighbour probably wondered why I was doing laundry all the time.

After all this I was pretty proud of myself, but you never know what a grow has in store for you. One day I came home to find the ebb and flow pump had malfunctioned and killed half the plants. All I could do was get some more clones and start over.

ALL THE F3 AND F4 seeds I produced at William Street went to Chris as a return on his investment in the grow. He sold them in his store and through his booming mail-order business, and began selling wholesale to seed banks that were popping up in other cities, like IRON in Toronto, Seeds Direct in Vancouver, and Crosstown Traffic in Ottawa. It was all part of "Overgrow the Government"—if everyone and their uncle grew pot, we figured it'd put more pressure on the government to relax its marijuana laws.

I started planting outdoor grows with the shit ton of leftover F1 and F2 seeds. I'd jump on my mountain bike and go for a ride and just scatter them, Johnny Appleseed style, in the forest or in abandoned fields. Outdoor grows have their own special challenges, one of which is deer. One night I thought it'd be cool if I jumped the fence of a wildlife sanctuary in a park and planted a single plant. It wasn't: a large buck showed up out of nowhere, reared up on its hind legs, and battered me with its hooves. I ran faster from it than I've ever run from police. You have to be careful harvesting outdoors—deer fucking love young cannabis, and the bucks *will* attack.

Sometimes my grows were a little more elaborate. Down on the shores of Lake Erie, near the town of Port Stanley, my friends and I would take a Zodiac out to little beaches that were only accessible by boat. We'd climb up the cliffs and plant right at the top, where the sun was good and it'd be hidden from passing boaters. It was a great idea until erosion became a factor. One year we lost twenty-plus feet off the cliff and suddenly my garden was on full display, our fifteen-foot sativas blowing in the breeze.

I grew anywhere, always trying to push the boundaries. I put pot plants in the window of my apartment. I put seedlings in the window of our head shop. There were big planters outside the main police station in London and outside city hall; I'd show up in the middle of the night and throw in some seeds.

I was so busy with Hemp Nation I hadn't found any traction with my photography career, so one day I looked through the help wanted ads and found a meat wholesaler called Hungry Howie's that needed a delivery guy. On hot summer days I'd go to the abattoirs and taste death in the air. It'd reek of blood, my sneakers stuck to the floor, there were fucking flies everywhere. It was the worst fucking job. It didn't help that I'd been a vegetarian since college.

My philosophy has always been that growing pot should never, ever, *ever* be a full-time job. If your whole life is growing and selling weed you *will* attract the wrong type of people, namely gangsters, criminals, and deadbeats. And when you're growing weed, anything can happen— you could get arrested, your plants could be stolen, a water pump might break—and bang, you gotta start over, and you need a fucking job to pay the bills while you grow out your next batch of cuttings.

But the biggest reason is psychological. Your plants are living entities and have a consciousness. If you do nothing but grow and sell pot, they'll know you're basically living off the avails of prostitution. If they sense they're being exploited, they'll do poorly. It's as simple as that.

You have to live in harmony with your plants. I call it The Green Triangle: it's you, your plants, and your pure intentions, and if you mess with any one of them, everything turns to shit.

6

THE
DOMINA
EFFECT

AFTER LIVING AT William Street for a year and a half, in 1995 I rented a house on Hill Street in the south part of London and converted the entire basement into a garden. Again, Chris subsidized the rent and the equipment. Hill Street was an even bigger, more professional grow, with three full rooms and eight 1,000-watt HID lamps. I had a single HID in the mother room, where I was growing a DMB plant, a Hindu Kush, and my signature strain, New York Skunk. In the vegetation room—which everyone calls the "veg" room—I grew out the cuttings under a pair of HIDs. Then they matured in the flowering room under the remaining five lights.

Since I was so involved in teaching—as the Minister of Agriculture, I designed and engineered gardens for people who came through Hemp Nation—I videotaped the entire build and showed it to people who wanted to start their own grow.

By this point I was mixing minerals and synthetic compounds to make my own nutrient supplements, and I was paying a lot of attention to the pH levels of the water. For the mother plants, I switched from an ebb and flow system to a deep water culture, a brand new hydroponic technique that has since become one of the most popular methods. Basically you just put the roots in water. One of the problems with ebb and flow is that your plants have water, then no water, then water again. With deep water culture you've got more stability: the root system is always submersed and exposed to whatever nutrients you're using.

The technical part is important, but I was also sure to spend quality time with my plants. They like it when you talk to them. They love it when you play music for them: I think they groove to the vibrations, just like humans do. I played a lot of jam bands when I gardened, like The String Cheese Incident, Fly Fantastic, and of course the Grateful Dead. Reggae was a given; back when I lived with Toast we listened to Bob Marley and Black Uhuru and Peter Tosh around the clock. And I was a skater and a surfer, so Slayer and Suicidal Tendencies were on the playlist as well.

Also, Madonna. People are always surprised that I like Madonna but I can't fucking help it—my love affair with her started back when I used to build ramps at skate parks; Christian Hosoi was one of the top skaters in the world and he loved Madonna, so I figured if she was good enough for him she was good enough for me.

The only problem with my new setup was electricity. Back on William Street, I was pulling 1,400 watts an hour, which was hardly noticeable in a building with other apartments. Hill Street was a single house drawing an extra 8,000 watts. The hydro company was sure to notice the spike in power and get suspicious. Even if they didn't, the hydro bills—which we called the Green Tax—would've put us under.

So I bypassed. I gave danger pay to an electrician friend named Furry to decouple the meter so I could draw juice directly from the grid.

I decided to watch him closely to see if I could learn to do it myself. I did learn two things. The first was that it's extremely fucking dangerous to bypass meters; if you're not a licensed electrician, you'll probably get yourself killed. The second was you can't reroute *all* of the juice around the meter or the hydro company will wonder why your usage has dropped to fucking *zero*. So Furry fixed it so that the massive amount of electricity used by the eight lamps wouldn't register, but all the other power I used would.

More than one grower has been busted when the hydro people noticed a massive uptick in an entire section of the grid, not just an individual house, but luckily I was around the corner from a church, a school, and the biggest hospital in London. The power uptick in that neighbourhood would never be noticed, which wouldn't be the case if I was growing in a lonely house out in the country.

While I was setting up Hill Street, Alan Young and Paul Burstein were busy assembling Chris's constitutional challenge, and telling him he had good reason to be optimistic. Hemp Nation was thriving despite the criminal charge hanging over Chris's head. The seed bank was growing by leaps and bounds—it'd become the biggest in Canada, if not North America—and we'd started an illegal after-hours café that served cannabis-laced drinks created by Andrew, our super talented and sometimes hot-headed Minister of Defence.

Every aspect of Hemp Nation was firing: retail was off the charts, our supply chain was solid, and it looked like we were actually going to dislodge Canada's drug laws.

And then I decided to grow a plant in my backyard.

I STILL ASK myself how I could've been so fucking stupid. I knew I wasn't doing anything morally wrong—the whole point of Hemp Nation was to challenge destructive and archaic marijuana laws—but the cops didn't see it that way yet and I already wore tie-dye and drove around in a truck decorated with a pot leaf, I didn't need to attract more attention. I must've got cocky from all my Overgrowing the Government. And part of me figured if I was ever arrested it'd just mean the Crown would have a second constitutional challenge on its hands.

But bottom line, I think I was just in love with this one particular plant, a gorgeous Black Domina. We'd discovered it in a catalogue from an Amsterdam seed company called Sensi Seeds, who gave it a sadomasochistic description that really intrigued us: "it'll leave you feeling wiped and beaten, with a strange smile on your face." I grew out a few plants indoors, and the strain turned out to be a stocky, dense, greasy indica that everyone loved since it was as strong as it was gnarly looking.

I've always liked pot grown outdoors—it has a different look and a different aroma—and I wanted to see how this gorgeous indica would do when exposed to natural elements. I figured since it was indica most people might not recognize it as cannabis—the iconic pot leaf is a sativa leaf, and indica leaves are smaller and more compact, with thick, dark petals. If you're not in the pot biz you might not even notice it *is* pot.

I planted a spare mother plant next to my composter, where it was partially hidden and I could run its water through the composter, dousing the plant with perfect, organic fertilizer. It came up right away. It got lots of sun and lots of water and when a pot plant is happy, it grows. I kept tying it down and still it hit nearly eight feet tall. I tied silk rose flowers onto the plant to throw off my neighbours. By the time I was finished, it pretty much looked like a massive rose bush—or at least I hoped it did, because there was a seven-storey apartment building right beside the yard.

The plant was almost mature when I came home one night and the thing was fucking *gone*.

My guess was someone with some knowledge of cannabis cultivation had been watching from the apartment building all along. I started watching the building, hunting for faces in windows or blinds going up or down—anything to tip off who might've been watching *me*. This went on for four days.

On the fifth day, I was home one afternoon when someone started knocking at the door. It was a drug squad officer. "I think," he said, "we need to talk about the plant in your backyard." We went around to the back and he pointed to what was left of the Domina, just a few branches at the bottom of the plant. That's when it hit me: whoever stole the plant had also called Crime Stoppers, meaning the thief not only had my Domina but $1,000 in reward money.

I was pissed as hell, though I tried not to show it. When talking to cops I was always courteous and cooperative. In fact, on the back of my Hemp Nation business card, which listed me as the Minister of Agriculture, there was a list of tips on how to deal with the police.

I said "yeah, I *had* a plant there, but someone stole it, and even though I know you're going to arrest me, I was wondering: Could I keep the main stock? There're no leaves or stems on it so it's not really a drug of any kind..."

"Alright," he said, shrugging.

I went into the house to get a green garbage bag. When I returned I found the officer standing in my doorway, sniffing. "You got weed in here?" he asked. "Because I can smell it."

I told him I'd just chopped a little to smoke a joint on my way to work. He told me that since I'd admitted to having drugs on the premises, he now had probable cause to come in and have a look around. (Word to the wise: never, ever admit to having drugs in your possession.) Still in the doorway, I told him he could take all the cannabis I had, just don't confiscate any of my glass pipes because one of them was made with the ashes of my friend who'd died.

"Alright," he said, and we went in. I told him my girlfriend had asthma and she smoked a little pot to stop attacks. I showed him a small Rubbermaid container with some ground-up pot in it, and a beautiful glass one-hitter, explaining how it only allowed her to take a very small amount at a time.

"This all there is?" he asked.

"Yeah," I told him, which was a *huge* fucking lie. There were a few ounces of Gold Seal hash in the coffee table drawer, which you could only see from the other side of the table, so I figured I'd get away with it. But he was standing next to the door of my office, where I had about thirty different strains of pot in labelled jars. And in the basement I had a few hundred plants, all nearing maturity with the aid of the most advanced growing equipment on the market. I'd recently harvested, and had about ten pounds of pot all packaged up and ready to go.

We went back outside and that's when he noticed the stairway leading to the basement. "What's down there?"

"Not sure," I told him. "The landlord keeps the door locked. I think he uses it for storage for his other properties."

"You sure?"

"I'm sure."

He nodded and went down the steps anyway and all I could think was, That's it, I'm fucked. He jiggled the door handle. Thank God I'd remembered to lock it.

He came back upstairs and we cut down the rest of the Domina. "You said you've got no idea what's down there?"

"None," I told him. "But listen, I know you're going to arrest me, do you mind if I just go inside and change and call my girlfriend?"

"You know what?" he said. "You've been cooperative, and it's just a tiny bit of weed, so I'm not gonna bust you." He left.

I was still standing there, my heart fucking pounding, when the little old lady from next door started calling, "Pete? Pete?"

At first I didn't even register, since everyone called me NY back then. Finally she got my attention. I looked over.

"Pete," she said, "what happened to your lovely rose bush?"

7

CRIMES OF COMPASSION

I REMEMBER THE first time I heard that pot could help sick people.

My brother, who's four years older than me, had severe asthma—he was always having life-threatening asthma attacks that'd land him in the hospital, and when he wasn't in the hospital he was constantly sucking on steroidal inhalers, which had a lot of side effects. One day when I was about eleven or twelve, my mother said she'd read about a new treatment for asthma: you steeped some pot in hot water, put a towel over your head, and let the steam fill your lungs.

My brother never tried it—which was strange since even back then I could've easily given him some weed—but I remember being struck by the idea that pot could be used for anything other than getting stoned.

WITH MY GARDEN, delivering meat for Hungry Howie's, and my duties at the store, I desperately needed help with the day-to-day gardening at the Hill Street grow. So Chris asked a good friend of ours, Gord, a skinny kid with bad skin, if he wanted to be involved. We all called him OG, though I was never sure whether it stood for "Original Gangster" or "Original Gord," or maybe something else altogether.

All I knew was that OG was the kindest, purest person I knew. I fucking loved the kid; I still tear up when I think of him. He had this loud, infectious cackle, particularly when he was stoned. He was popular around the Nation since he was always so upbeat. Nobody would've blamed him if he weren't—he was born with cystic fibrosis, and was so sick as a baby he spent the first year or two of his life in the hospital. The doctors told his parents he wouldn't see fourteen years old.

He was about eighteen when he came into Hemp Nation one day to buy some seeds. He started talking with Chris, and told him something interesting: when he smoked pot it seemed to dry up all the fluid in his lungs, which meant he could cough it up and breathe easier.

It made sense that he be part of the Hill Street garden: he was always at the hospital around the corner, so it was convenient for him to take a walk and do some gardening before he had to go back for his treatments. I'd come home from work and there he'd be, still in his hospital gown and hooked up to his oxygen machine. And he'd be laughing away, happier than any of us have a right to be, positive proof that cannabis has some interesting medical, as well as spiritual, benefits.

When I saw how OG benefitted from marijuana smoking, something clicked in me. *This* is what I would do.

My focus shifted away from recreational cannabis use and toward the struggle to liberalize Canada's laws around medical cannabis use. The way I saw it, recreational pot smokers had various organizations to fight for them, like Hemp Nation, the Marijuana Party, and NORML (the National Organization for the Reform of Marijuana Laws). Yet the idea that marijuana could help sick people was relatively new, and few people were fighting for it.

My new interest was only strengthened by customers I met at the store: people used cannabis to fight the wasting syndrome caused by HIV infection, or to control the motor dysfunction of multiple sclerosis, or to fight the nausea that comes with chemotherapy. A guy named Jeff had really bad Crohn's disease, and found that smoking pot helped with pain and weight management.

Some of the people I met couldn't work and had a hard time affording their pot, so I decided to sell a portion of the Hill Street grow to medical users at $3.50 a gram instead of the usual $7. I also decided to sell only small amounts to compassion clients, since I didn't want them buying cheap from me and then selling it on the street. So I started riding my bike around with a knapsack filled with a little scale and jars of different strains, and that's how the London Cannabis Compassion Centre (or LCCC) was born.

Soon after, I helped found a group called the Medical Marijuana Centres of Ontario (MMCO), which was an umbrella group to represent all the compassion centres that were popping up around this time. We had groups from Kitchener, Etobicoke, and Ottawa, a pair from

Peterborough, and a pair from Toronto: Cannabis as Living Medicine (CALM), and the Toronto Compassion Centre
(TCC), which operated from a little room on Church Street.

Meeting these people strengthened my commitment to
medical marijuana even more. In the pot business you met
some cool people, but you also met a lot of super sketchy
fuckheads. The members of the MMCO were all good, kind,
brave, smart people, and I remember really hoping they'd
all see me the same way.

The first thing we did was write a letter to Allan Rock,
the health minister at the time, calling on him to officially
recognize what we were doing. When he didn't respond we
decided to hold a press conference.

We rented a small hall on Church Street, in the heart
of Toronto's gay village: a high number of medical users
were HIV positive, so there was a lot of support in the gay
community for legal medical marijuana. Representatives from all the compassion groups were there, as well
as Alan Young, our lawyer from the Hemp Nation trial.
In the audience were medical users, members of the public who were concerned about the issue, reporters, and a
few police.

Warren Hitzig, a former skateboard and snowboard
champion who was one of the operators of the TCC, did
most of the talking. He was on the front lines of the fight
to legalize medical marijuana, and was an effective
spokesperson. His speech was short and to the point—he
announced the existence of the MMCO, noted that the use
of marijuana for compassionate purposes was illegal and
that we'd received no assistance or acknowledgement from
either Health Canada or our Minister of Health, and vowed

that MMCO members would work as hard as possible to ensure that ill clients could receive medical marijuana.

WE HELD REGULAR meetings, almost always in Toronto. The other members quickly convinced me that the LCCC should have a brick-and-mortar headquarters so we wouldn't be mistaken for a thinly disguised street dealer— some people thought that compassion centres were run by dealers looking for a way around the current laws.

Before taking the next step I wanted an actual medicinal marijuana user to officially represent the LCCC. So I talked to Lynn Harichy, an LCCC client with multiple sclerosis who weighed about ninety-seven pounds at the time. She smoked a couple grams of my weed each day to control all shaking and bladder problems that came with her disease. I liked Lynn, and suggested she become the figurehead for the LCCC. I also told her I hoped that, when we managed to rent an actual store, she'd put her name on the lease, even though I would pay the rent and all the bills.

She agreed on both counts and I started taking her to meetings of the umbrella group in Toronto. Her husband, a scrawny little weasel named Mike, insisted on coming as well, and that's when the problems started.

Right from the start I didn't like the guy, mostly because of how he treated Lynn on the drive to Toronto: he was always putting her down, always degrading her, never letting her talk. It soon got to the point I didn't even want to go when he came along, so I started driving by myself.

Also, he was always bugging me to sell him more and more pot at the reduced, compassion price. He didn't have much of a job—I think he worked part-time at a truck stop—and I just knew he wanted to start dealing Lynn's compassion pot. I'd tell him, "no man, it doesn't work that way," and he'd be like "no, no, I got a buddy with MS," so I'd tell him as soon as that "buddy" got a doctor's note he could come and buy directly from me.

That shut Mike up for a bit, but then it started up again.

"Come on NY, you gotta sell us more, Lynn's really sick, and I've got this buddy who's suffering, so just lay a *few* more grams on me..."

I refused. I could not fucking believe he was trying to make money off his dying wife.

AFTER A COUPLE months of this, Mike and Lynn found a little storefront in a sketchy neighbourhood on Wellington Street. It was dirty and rundown and there was no space for clients to hang out. I didn't like it.

I told them I wanted someplace better, downtown. Again, it was Mike who did all the talking, saying if I wanted Lynn's name on the lease then I had to go with the place they wanted. In the end I agreed. I shouldn't have, but I did. At least the place was fucking cheap, like $300 a month.

So now the LCCC had its own headquarters, and I was no longer riding around town on my mountain bike with a big bag of weed and a scale. This is what I focused on: the LCCC was up and running. Maybe there were some problems with it, but who gives a shit? There always *are* problems in the dope world.

IT WAS AN exciting time. The Hemp Nation family may have seemed like a ragtag bunch of stoner kids—except for a few of the LCCC clients, none of us were over twenty-five, and some of us were much younger—yet we were fighting the unjust criminalization of marijuana on several fronts.

First, there was Hemp Nation, as in Hemp Nation the store, Hemp Nation the mail-order business, and Hemp Nation the activist movement. When we first started the seed bank, we fit all our seeds in a two-by-two-foot box. Now, we had a full-on menu with thirty or forty different strains. Our client list for mail-order seeds was growing each day, helping create private gardens to Overgrow the Government all over Canada.

Then there was the constitutional challenge. It still hadn't gone to trial, but we'd found more than a dozen expert witness who had agreed to testify about the low health risks of cannabis, or the ills brought on by prohibition, or the costs associated with enforcement.

Finally, there was my new compassion movement and all of its highly sympathetic users. *Surely*, we thought, something would soon give.

In September of 1995, almost two years after the raid on The Great Canadian Hemporium, the Crown offered Chris Clay a plea bargain: if he pleaded guilty to minor possession, they'd drop the other charges.

Chris called a meeting of the Hemp Nation family to ask us if we thought he should take the plea. My guess is he'd made up his mind up already, and just wanted to hear it from us as well. Of course we were all like, "fuck no, after two years they offer a plea *now*?" Clearly, we figured, they thought they were going to lose. So Chris called his lawyer, who told the Crown the answer was no.

The very next day, the cops raided Hemp Nation.

THE
OTHER CHEEK

IT HAPPENED SHORTLY after the store opened at eleven in the morning. Five drug squad officers came in, each wearing cargo pants and RCMP jackets and fucking bulletproof vests. A new employee named Sarah Delaney was working the counter that day.

"Can I help you?" she asked.

"Not really," one of them said. "You're under arrest."

They made her sit in the corner while they searched the store. As Sarah watched, they carted away every bong, every pipe, every how-to manual, every pair of striped hemp pants, every joss stick and Bob Marley T-shirt and jade amulet and black-light poster.

When they were done the store was practically empty. Then they led Sarah, uncuffed at least, to a paddy wagon in the back lane and took her to the London Police Service headquarters (the only police station in town), where they finger-printed her, questioned her, and detained her in a holding cell. They charged her with three counts of possession—one for seeds and two for paraphernalia—and, since she worked in a store that sold cannabis seeds, one count of drug trafficking.

Meanwhile, the drug squad guys went to Chris's house and arrested him in front of his parents. He'd stopped smoking pot by then, but they searched his room and found a tiny amount of hash that he must've forgotten about. They took him to the station and charged him with the same offences as Sarah, plus an additional possession charge for the hash.

When I found out later that day that Chris had gotten busted again, and that they'd taken Sarah as well, my immediate reaction was, "you have *got* to be fucking kidding me." *I* was the Minister of Agriculture, the one who taught pot growing every Sunday, the one whose picture was on our flyer that said "learn how to grow cannabis from Canadian cultivator NYPD." I even had a strain named after me: NYPD Green. Yet they didn't even question me—instead they went after Sarah, a part-timer who just wanted to make some extra money for school.

That night I ended up walking around the police station looking in windows, trying to spot Chris or Sarah. I was outraged the police would hit so hard beneath the belt. As strange as this sounds, we always had a good relationship with the cops, or at least the cops in London. We were always nice to them, and there were many times they cut us a break.

One night after the shop closed, a bunch of us were having a major smoke-a-thon in the office behind the store when the door buzzer sounded. Chris went down to answer it and there was the local beat cop. He said he wasn't going to arrest anybody, but he wanted to come up and give us a warning. So he came up to the office. We looked at him, he looked at us, and then he said, "guys, c'mon, close the fucking *window*." We had accidentally left it wide open; people could probably smell the weed half a mile away.

That's how it was between the police and us. Everyone understood it was just pot. It wasn't PCP or crystal meth, it wasn't hurting anyone; all we did was have drum circles in the park and spread peace, love, and Oreo cookies. There was an understanding: we didn't like the dope laws and they didn't like enforcing them, so we were all in a difficult situation together.

When they busted Chris the first time we were like, "okay, you had to do this, we get it, we're going to take the opportunity to launch a challenge and maybe we'll get this whole ridiculous situation figured out." But I guess they saw it differently.

By busting Chris after he turned down the plea bargain, it was obvious the police and the Crown were punishing him for not playing ball. And to go after Sarah instead of me? Maybe we were being paranoid and it was just because she happened to be in the store during the raid, but we figured they thought she was Chris's girlfriend and they wanted to use her as leverage against him.

Now it felt personal. Everyone in Hemp Nation started to question any respect they had for the local police.

THEY RELEASED SARAH the next morning, and later they dropped the charges against her. Chris they kept all weekend, just like after the first bust, and on Monday morning a Justice of the Peace released him on a $50,000 bond—ten times the bond he'd posted after his first arrest.

As a condition of release, the store had to stop selling anything even the slightest bit illegal; in other words, all the stuff that provided most of his revenue. No more seeds, no more pipes, no more bongs, no more how-to books—he couldn't even sell fucking rolling papers or the cops would arrest him again for paraphernalia, and then his bail would go up, and he'd have to siphon even *more* money away from his defence fund.

With all of his bestselling stock gone, Chris was now saddled with a lease on a store that was mostly empty. Hemp Nation became a hemp clothing store. Sales fell off a cliff. I'd recently quit delivering meat for Hungry Howie's so I could focus on Overgrowing the Government. Now, Chris had to cut my Hemp Nation hours so much that I was forced to call up Hungry Howie's and ask for my fucking job back.

Chris had been keeping Hemp Nation afloat for two years while simultaneously funding a constitutional challenge to the criminal code, but as anyone who's ever run a store knows, retail is a tough business at the best of times. This second arrest hurt.

THOUGH CONSERVATIVE IN some ways, London was a pot-friendly town. In addition to the Hemp Nation family, there were tons of hippies and pot smokers and girls in flowery dresses and guys with dreads and sandals. On April 28, 1997, we all piled into the Middlesex County Court House, so many of us that some had to sit on the floor, to witness the case of *Christopher James Clay v. Her Majesty the Queen.*

The judge was an old guy named John F. McCart who was hearing his last trial before retirement. The day started with some dull procedural bullshit. Eventually the prosecutor, a guy named William Buchner, motioned for a recess. The judge broke for lunch and we all filed out.

When we returned for the afternoon session the door to the courtroom was locked. The bailiff told me there were too many of us, and due to fire regulations we weren't allowed in. I looked in the window and saw there were lots of empty seats. I told him it was our civic right to be inside. He let in ten people, including me, and it didn't take me long to figure that it was Buchner who'd complained about us overcrowding the courtroom.

I stood up right beside Buchner and said, "Listen up people! There're some people here who don't want all of Chris's supporters in the courtroom, but as long as there are seats they *have* to let us in. So everybody move over, love your neighbour, one-cheek it if you have to..."

Everyone squished in, so the bailiff let in ten more, and ten more, and ten more, and the whole time Buchner was fucking *fuming*. By the time the afternoon session started, we were all squeezed in and there was nothing he could do.

OVER THE NEXT two weeks we heard all of the expert witnesses brought in by Young and Burstein. We had a farmer who talked about the benefits of hemp as an agricultural product. There was a psychiatrist who testified that pot wasn't addictive, and he debunked the idea that pot use leads to harder drugs. We had a professor of statistics talk about the extreme costs of enforcing our drug laws, and a criminology professor from BC who told the court that Canadian drug laws were first drafted to oppress Asian immigrants at the turn of the century. There was another psychiatrist, who testified that cannabis could be used medicinally for many illnesses; his testimony was followed by Lynn Harichy, who described how pot helped with her MS symptoms, and another LCCC client named Brenda Rochford, who used weed to help with something called Ehlers-Danlos syndromes, a horrible condition that fucks with your connective tissue. We had a doctor up from New York who testified how safe pot was compared to other drugs; he kept using the phrase "on par with caffeine." We even had a psychiatry prof from fucking Harvard Medical School fly up to testify on Chris's behalf.

The cost of all the witnesses' travel, food, and accommodation was covered by Chris's legal defence fund. It somehow became my job to take care of them while they were in town, I think because I was the only one with a vehicle. If they needed food in the middle of the night, I'd go pick it up for them. If they needed something from the liquor store, I'd deliver it. If they needed to go somewhere, I'd drive them.

And if they needed some weed—sativa, indica, hash, edibles, whatever their pleasure—I'd give it to them on the house. I was their man.

I don't think any of the witnesses actually testified high, but there was one guy with a bad back who was on the stand for a full day and a half; he kept having to stand to feel more comfortable, and he told me that every time he did he smelled weed. He'd be testifying away, thinking, "Jesus Christ, who was stupid enough to bring marijuana into a court of law? And why am I only smelling it when I stand up?"

Eventually he realized that he was that stupid person: I'd brought him some pot the night before his first day on the stand, and he'd put in the front pocket of his sports coat and forgotten about it. Every time he stood up his pocket would open slightly and release the scent of that fresh, gooey nug. Till this day, I wonder if the judge ever caught a whiff.

DURING THE WHOLE two-week trial, the prosecution brought in exactly two witnesses. The first was an old guy from the Addiction Research Foundation who testified that smoking marijuana was carcinogenic and detrimental to your health. Yet under further questioning, he admitted there was no firm evidence of a link between pot smoking and cancer, that it was more of a presumed risk. Their second witness was some fire chief who claimed, based on an actual fire he'd attended, that private gardens could cause electrical shorts that could lead to fires. Upon cross-examination he admitted that the fire he cited had actually started in the grower's kitchen, and had nothing to do with the garden itself.

In his closing statement, Alan Young said he hoped he'd provided "effective tools to be a vehicle for the change." When Young was finished, Buchner stood up and said that marijuana was a gateway to harder drugs, and a law was a

law whether you liked it or not, and that law had been broken by one Christopher J. Clay.

Then it was over. We all filed out, thinking there was no
way we could lose.

The judge went away for almost three months. Court
resumed on August 14 to hear the judgement. We all
squeezed in again, feeling confident. McCart started by
telling the court that he'd learned a lot during the proceed-
ings and he agreed that marijuana was relatively harm-
less. He accepted that Chris was selling seeds not to profit
from the "illicit black market" but to challenge the laws—
"Mr. Clay genuinely believes the harshness of marijuana
laws needs to be alleviated or eased"—and he agreed that
the laws should probably be reconsidered. We were cheering, silently, since we knew, we just fucking *knew*, he was
going to accept the challenge and free Chris.

But then, he didn't. We all gasped.

McCart said that although he agreed with the defence's
claims, he felt it should be legislatures that change marijuana laws and not the courts. That was complete bullshit;
we knew there were ample precedents for courts changing the law. We couldn't fucking believe it. We filed out,
reporters were everywhere. Chris was mobbed.

Me and a bunch of Hemp Nationals went to the store
and grabbed our Hemp Nation street sign and a chain.
Then we marched back to the courthouse and fastened it
to the handrails on the front steps. We were so pissed we
were going to set it on fire. Luckily, Alan Young talked
some sense into my pissed-off brain.

A few weeks after that, court convened once more for
the sentencing. McCart gave Chris a $750 fine, permanently

confiscated the $80,000 worth of inventory the cops had taken, and imposed probation to be served in a different province. So that's what it came down to: no time served, but his store was gutted and he was run out of town.

With cash so tight while he fought this case, he'd laid off most of his staff. He'd tried rebranding as the Hemp Nation Café, serving healthy, organic food, but it just didn't fly. For two years, it'd been Chris who locked up, Chris who mopped the floors, Chris who cleaned the bathrooms and manned the till and dealt with customers. Chris was exhausted.

So he moved to the coast of British Columbia. He started doing web design and development, a skill he'd learned while fundraising for his defence. He also started working with the British Columbia Compassion Club Society and ended up on their board of directors. His story was later covered on an episode of *The Nature of Things* with David Suzuki, whose parents, apparently, lived just down the street from Chris.

In many ways, Chris and I have since come full circle; in the fall of 2016, he and I opened up the Warmland Compassion Centre out on Vancouver Island. Naturally, he did it all in his own unique Chris way; he bought highway billboard ads to promote the sale of cannabis years before anyone else dared.

But first—before paying his fine, leaving for the coast, and getting married and having three kids—he did one very important thing, at least from my perspective.

He let me take over Hemp Nation.

I GROW
POT HERE!

THE FIRST THING I did was change the name to The Organic Traveller. "Hemp Nation" had served its purpose, and I wanted to blaze my own path. The name came from a phrase I used back then (and still do): "Don't panic, it's all organic." Also, I wanted to take the words "cannabis" or "pot" or "hemp" out of the name, to remove the drug culture connotations and instead suggest something healthy and pure. Next, I restocked the pipes and bongs—the judge had told *Chris* he couldn't sell them, not me.

My big problem at the time was competition from a shop called Hi-Times. They'd opened at our old address on King Street, and often our distributors would go to Hi-Times thinking it was still us and we'd just changed our name. There weren't yet catalogues or websites to order paraphernalia from; your distributors would just pull up with a trunk full of hookahs and bongs and patchouli or whatever.

They'd go in to Hi-Times and discover it wasn't us at all, but Hi-Times would tell them Chris had been busted for selling hard drugs, or Hemp Nation had gone out of business, or whatever they needed to say to make it look like they were the only game in town. They even put up a sign claiming to be the "first and finest" head shop in London, which was complete horseshit since that title belonged to The Great Canadian Hemporium.

I made a point of selling only quality, locally produced equipment. If it wasn't from London I made sure it was from Ontario, and if it wasn't from Ontario I made sure it was from Canada. Slowly, London-area pot smokers started to realize we were again selling quality pipes and bongs, and they didn't have to deal with the assholes at Hi-Times to get them.

People responded and soon the store, under its new name, was making money again.

THE SUCCESS OF the store let me turn my attention to the London Cannabis Compassion Centre. Just before the trial we'd set up in the Wellington Street storefront that Lynn and Mike Harichy had found, and since then things had gone from bad to worse.

Mike kept pestering me for more and more weed at the medical rate, and I kept saying, "Mike, for fuck's sake, it doesn't work that way." I could tell by the look in his eyes he wasn't listening.

The LCCC was only supposed to sell to people with a doctor's certificate, but I started hearing rumours that Mike was selling to anyone who came to the fucking door. I don't know how many times I told him that if we were

going to be taken seriously we *had* to document everything we did. Every time, the same old bullshit: me saying,
"Mike, you gotta stop, you can't sell to that guy," and him
being like, "Don't worry, I know him, he's really sick, and
by the way can you give me some more?"

I thought about cutting him off. But I felt bad for Lynn
and her children. MS affects people in different ways; it
made Lynn's nerves fire so that she shook horribly, sometimes so much that she couldn't control her bladder or
bowels. Pot took all of that away. She could've got it someplace else, but there was no one else in London who would
sell it to her for just $3.50 a gram.

And because Mike didn't work, or didn't work *much*,
they didn't have much money. This was a huge source of
conflict between the two of them. It was also the reason I
was confident he was reselling my cheap pot on the street
for the going rate of $7 a gram.

Things came to a head the next time the three of us
attended a meeting of the Medical Marijuana Centres of
Ontario. It was at a head shop called the Toronto Hemp
Company on Yonge Street, just south of Bloor. Lynn was
quiet, like she always was around Mike, while we all talked
about dispensing weed.

And then suddenly she blew up, yelling that I was
always trying to control things and I was always trying to
control *her* and that if it didn't stop she was fucking going
to kill me. Lynn was practically crying she was so upset.

Everyone else was stone silent, just looking at her
thinking "where did this come from, Lynn's always so
quiet and polite..." And there was Mike beside her, grinning like a Cheshire fucking cat.

He'd put her up to it. I fucking *knew* it. He wasn't getting anywhere with me so he persuaded her to do something about it, and when she finally did she exploded. All
that frustration about her disease, and her shit marriage,
and her husband taking her medicine—which was probably
why she'd been looking so thin and pale—it all came surg-
ing up and she couldn't control it.

I told her she was cut off. I felt bad and did it anyway.
I also told them I was done with the LCCC, and that they
could have the name and the organization as long as it
didn't involve me.

Three months later they were arrested at the LCCC for
selling pot to an undercover police officer. Of course, the
headlines were terrible—"Medicinal Marijuana Dispensary Sells Pot to Undercover Cop"—and confirmed a lot of
people's beliefs that the compassion movement was just
another form of dealing.

And everyone knew the LCCC was my baby, so reporters
were calling me up and asking questions about the arrest
and each time I had to say that I was out of it and that the
LCCC was not representative of me or the compassion
movement. I said I supported the police in targeting anyone who uses sick people to make money.

Lynn passed away a few years later. Mike Harichy might
still be around, though the last time I saw him on the street
he looked strung out and borderline homeless. If that's not
karma I don't know what is.

AFTER LEAVING THE LCCC I formed the London Compassion Society, or the LCS, which I operated out of The

Organic Traveller. Every night at six I'd close up shop and wait for people to knock on the front door. I'd peer through a peephole, and if the person held up a card showing he or she was a registered user, I'd let them in and sell them their meds. At nine o'clock or so I'd call it a day and head home.

Word got around and strangers soon started showing up at the LCS claiming to be sick, but I insisted on only selling to *registered* users. I figured if I sold to just anyone I'd be no better than a regular street dealer. Also, I was selling at half the price of pot on the street; I had to be sure my clients deserved that discount.

If you had a doctor's note prescribing the use of marijuana, you could register with Health Canada as a medical user and then legally buy pot from what's known as an "Authorized Licensed Producer of Cannabis for Medical Purposes," or as most people called it, a "Licensed Producer." There was a catch, though—it was extremely expensive and time consuming to become a Licensed Producer. There were literally years' worth of applications involved, and you had to build a state-of-the-art, super high-end facility with rigorous hygiene and security, all of which was super fucking expensive. As a result there weren't many Licensed Producers, no more than a handful in all of Canada. So medical users bought cannabis from people like me, who operated on the dark side of a grey market.

A lot of my potential clients didn't know how to register, so to help them I teamed up with the Toronto Compassion Centre. Back then it was run by two guys. The first was Warren Hitzig, the guy who had done most of the talking at the Church Street press conference. The second was a cannabis entrepreneur named Dom Cramer. He went on to run a bunch of Toronto businesses like Vapor Central, Kindred Cafe, Sacred Seeds—he was a brilliant guy who positioned himself perfectly in Toronto's thriving cannabis community.

The TCC was much bigger and more organized than I was. They had something I could only *dream* of: staff. So we struck a deal. When a prospective client came to the LCS, the TTC would do all the paperwork to register them. In return, I supplied the TTC with pot I'd grown in London. It was a good arrangement, though at first I felt like they were doing a lot more for me than I was for them. That would soon change.

ONE DAY WARREN called me to ask for a favour. He told me about a member of the TCC, an eighteen-year-old kid named Andrew who lived with severe epilepsy. The poor kid had once had a seizure while holding a pair of scissors and almost taken his eye out. But cannabis almost eliminated his seizures, to the point that he stopped taking his epilepsy medicine, which had never really worked in the first place.

Cannabis worked so well that Andrew had started to grow his own, and it looked like he had a bit of a green thumb. The problem was that he was selling to the wrong sort of people. He lived with his dysfunctional mother and sister, and the whole family wasn't doing well—bills weren't being paid, they were facing eviction, they weren't eating right. It sounded to me like the whole family was hanging on by a thread.

Warren told me his plan: they'd move the family to London, to get the kid away from the criminals he'd starting running with in Toronto. "And once he's there," Warren asked, "maybe you could look out for him?" I said yes.

So they moved to London.

I REMEMBER MEETING them for the first time. Andrew was a scrawny kid with a bit of an edge to him, though I felt like that came from the people he'd been hanging with in Toronto and didn't reflect the person he was inside. His sister was quiet and reclusive: whenever I dropped by she'd be watching TV or reading a magazine. Though his mother was super nice, she always seemed frazzled, forever apologizing about the way she looked or what a mess the apartment was or how she wished she had something to offer me to drink.

I helped Andrew set up a small, two-lamp grow in the basement of the apartment they were renting. In return, he agreed to sell all his cannabis to the London Compassion Society, and I would then distribute it to medical users.

There was one problem: Andrew and his mother were terrible with money. If you gave them a dollar they'd spend it immediately. If you gave them $1,000 it'd be gone by the end of the day. Andrew loved candy: he'd walk into a store and drop $100 on chocolate bars and Vachon cakes and fucking gummy bears.

So we came up with a plan. Let's say the LCS bought $2,000 worth of pot from him. I knew if I gave him that money in a lump sum, it'd be gone the next day. So I gave them a weekly allowance, enough for rent, utilities, groceries, and some spending money, and spread it out so that it lasted until the next growth cycle was finished. For a while this worked out, and his family wasn't broke like they'd been back in Toronto.

One day I went to pick up my usual two pounds, only this time he said he'd had a bad harvest, and only had a pound and a half to give me. At first I believed him, until I noticed a huge fucking pile of candy in the corner. That's when I knew he was selling out the back door of his apartment, most likely to the sort of people he'd been selling to back in Toronto. When I confronted him he denied it, and claimed he'd just had a bad harvest. The next time it was just over a pound, and the time after that it was down to a single pound.

He'd gotten a taste for the money. It happens. Of all the things that can go wrong with an illegal grow—theft, police seizures, dead plants, suspicious landlords—the worst by far is greed. It makes the grower take stupid risks. Once that happens there's no going back.

So I cut Andrew off. I told him the LCS was no longer going to buy any of his cannabis, and I'd no longer give his family an allowance. He didn't seem bothered by it.

Soon I heard he'd hooked up with a black-market dealer, an old friend of mine called Eggie. Eggie moved Andrew out of the apartment and gave him a huge grow in a farmhouse out near Goderich. Now, Andrew was an eighteen-year-old kid living alone on a farm in the middle of nowhere with a fucking pitbull for protection—he might as well have put a neon sign on the roof saying "I Grow Pot Here!"

I knew it was only a matter of time before they got busted and all of their plants were seized. This was a problem for me: I'd let Andrew grow out a beautiful Skunk No. 1 mother plant of mine, and it was now at the Goderich farmhouse.

When I told Eggie I wanted my mother plant back, he said he'd get it for me if he could use my pickup truck to do it. I agreed, but only if Andrew didn't get in the truck: the kid had bad energy and I figured if he was involved they'd get caught. Eggie and I met that afternoon in a little town just north of London and traded vehicles. I should've wondered why he wanted to use my truck instead of his own, but I'd soon find out.

He told me he'd see me in an hour and a half. He left. Two hours went by. I called him and there was no answer. Then four hours went by, then six. Finally I went to bed.

The next day, at six thirty in the morning, someone started pounding on my door. I looked out, and there was Andrew. I was so fucking pissed I didn't answer. He left, and I found a note on the door that read: "Arrested last night, your truck was impounded and the truck you're driving is stolen. Sorry."

Later that day I pieced together what'd happened. Eggie had realized the heat was on the farmhouse—a fucking Ontario Provincial Police officer lived one line over, something he hadn't bothered to check when he rented the place—so instead of using my truck to return my mother plant like he fucking *said* he would, he used it to move 450 pot plants to a different location. And the morons waited until the middle of the night to do it, breaking the cardinal rule: don't do shit in the middle of the night, when the only other people on the road are the fucking police. The cops picked them up driving through downtown Goderich.

My truck was still registered to my father, so that afternoon the Ontario Provincial Police showed up at his house in St. Thomas to question him about his involvement in a grow operation they'd just seized in Goderich. He called me while they were searching his house. He was freaking out, so I booked it down there.

I told the OPP that I was the one who'd lent the truck to Greg—"yes sir, that's his real name but everyone calls him Eggie"—and that he'd told me he was going to move a couch and "no sir, I didn't know anything about marijuana plants, if I had I'd *never* have lent him the truck." On and on I went, spouting all this bullshit, until finally the OPP officer threw up his hands and said, "alright already, enough." He left.

It took my dad six months to get the truck from the impound lot. Eggie got six months in jail and Andrew got probation.

I lost one of my favourite mother plants, as well as something far more important: at the time, I had wild grows in forests and fields all around London, and underneath the front seat of the truck was a GPS unit containing the location of each of those grows. The police took it as evidence, meaning they'd probably already sent agents out to destroy the crops, or were watching them in case someone was stupid enough to show up to harvest. Either way, I'd lost my entire outdoor crop that year, and all because I'd fallen in love with that beautiful Skunk No. 1 plant . . .

NOW THAT THE TCC was registering my clients, the LCS was growing. First I had five clients, then ten, then fifteen. As word got round, my client list grew exponentially. I had clients with cancer, with epilepsy, with muscular dystrophy, with glaucoma and Parkinson's and postoperative pain and HIV and Crohn's disease and depression and migraines and arthritis and neurodegenerative disorders I'd never even fucking *heard* of. They all seemed to genuinely benefit from smoking pot, or at least they were able to get a certificate saying that they did.

Not only did I have to come up with enough pot to sell to them, I'd also promised to sell a bunch to Warren and Dom at the TCC. I needed more pot.

On the supply side, I still had my Hill Street grow, and I was helping with a bunch of other private grows in exchange for the gardeners providing pot to the LCS. On the downside, I'd lost every one of my own outdoor grows thanks to Andrew and Eggie being complete fuckheads. There were plenty of black-market growers, but some had weapons and protection animals and criminal ties, so I only bought from them when I had no choice.

My only option was to replace my lost outdoor grows. I was working sixty hours a week at The Organic Traveller, and spending the rest of my time doling out medical pot at the LCS or tending to the gardens I already had; I didn't have time to set up another indoor grow like Hill Street. Outdoor grows don't take a lot of time: you plant a bunch of cuttings in the late spring, and you show up in the fall to harvest. They also give you a reason to get outdoors, and with all the time I was spending in the store I needed that.

The problem with outdoor gardens is the loss rate. Your plants get stolen by pot hunters or damaged by storms or they die during dry spells or drug enforcement officers find them. Or, most likely, stoner-ass deer eat them.

Full-time outdoor growers deal with this by planting everywhere. There was an outdoor grower in London called Special Ed who made sure that every patch of forest, pasture, and corn field within a hundred miles of London had some of his cannabis growing in it. He'd hire entire fucking *crews* of planters, outfit them with headlamps and trays of seedlings and night-lights, and they'd plant night after night. At harvest time he might only get one out of ten plants back, but since he'd planted so much it was enough for him to make a living.

I didn't have the time for that so I turned to that tried-and-true friend of the guerrilla outdoor grower.

The cornfield.

TWELVE OR TWENTY-FOUR

THE FIRST DRUG LAWS in Canada weren't intended to reduce drug use. Instead, as I learned at Chris's trial, they were aimed at under-the-table Chinese factory workers who were supposedly taking jobs away from Canadians. Since opium was their drug of choice, all opium-based drugs were criminalized around the turn of the century. Cocaine followed in 1911, and in 1918 Canada nearly outlawed alcohol.

In the early 1920s, a woman named Emily Murphy (Canada's first female judge) wrote *The Black Candle*, the first book published in Canada to demonize pot use. She claimed that smoking the dried leaves of marijuana caused insanity, rape, and murder, which was not only ridiculous but ill-informed: there's virtually no drug in the leaves. Still, the book caught on—it was serialized in

Maclean's—and in 1923 a federal bill criminalizing marijuana passed without opposition. It was a weird law to pass, seeing as no one smoked back then. They didn't convict anyone under the new law for fourteen years.

Pot was outlawed on May 3, 1923, and I'd bet that by May 4 people were planting cannabis seedlings in cornfields.

Mostly, it's about convenience: cornfields are fucking *everywhere*. It's also about size: the fields are often hundreds and hundreds of hectares, so it's easy to hide a few plants without the farmer ever knowing.

I'd never been that big on cornfields myself, though. I didn't want to worry about farmers catching me; it's a small worry since farmers aren't out in the middle of the night when most guerrilla planting gets done, but it's a worry you don't have if you're just scattering seeds in a forest somewhere. Also, you never know if or when a farmer is going to spray weedkiller, and I've never been wild about the idea of harvesting pot that's been treated with Roundup. And in order to plant your weed cuttings you first have to tear out a bunch of corn stalks, which always struck me as bad karma: if you destroy Plant A to grow Plant B, Plant B will sense it and not do as well.

The biggest problem with cornfield grows is the goddamn pot thieves. In Canada, there's a multi-million-dollar pot theft industry, and in the United States that figure is probably in the billions. The first place thieves hunt for pot is in cornfields: they'd come to Southwestern Ontario, rent a plane, tell the pilot they were looking for property or doing a study on corn growth or some bullshit, then fly a grid pattern and look for huge, bright-green patches inside the fields. So if you were a dedicated cornfield grower, you had to go big, and accept that the majority of your cannabis wouldn't be there when you went to harvest.

DESPITE ALL THE drawbacks, I guess when I found myself with the opportunity it was just too tempting to pass up.

By this time I'd moved to a farmhouse on a country lane outside of London called Twelve Mile Road. I lived there with four other people who were all involved with the cannabis trade, including my girlfriend, Artemis. I'd met her at one of the drum circles I hosted in the back of The Organic Traveller during the winter. She owned a VW bus and wore dreadlocks and sewed her clothes from patches of leftover material; I don't think I'd ever met anyone who was such a full-on hippie. Right across the field from our house was a grass field, and beyond that was an enormous cornfield.

The first thing I had to do was make sure it was feed corn, not sweet corn, which is harvested too early for my plants to mature. I found the information signpost—every cornfield has one—on the opposite side of the field and looked up the code online. I was in luck.

I waited until the corn plants reached a certain height: corn farmers use an oil-based fertilizer that kills cannabis, so you can only plant when the corn is mature enough that its fertilization cycle is over. You can get a pretty good idea when this is by doing some research on the strain of corn being grown. Or, if you happen to live next door like I did, you can just look out your window and watch for them spraying.

I went deep into the field and planted four plants in between two rows, so I wouldn't have to tempt karma by killing any of the corn. Plus I figured my plants would be harder to detect. Then I pruned the surrounding corn stalks so that my plants would have more sun and air. Then I moved to a different location in the same field and planted four more, and then four more, and so on until I had twenty-four plants in the ground. I used a pattern, so that as long as I found one patch I could find them all— my favourite number is twelve, so I'd always walk either twelve or twenty-four steps.

Then I waited. I knew the harvest date of my field— again, from the signpost—and the trick is to harvest as close to that date as you can. You want your plants to mature as much as possible without the fucking farmer tearing them down for you.

My plan was to harvest in mid-October. One morning in early October, I woke up early and saw a fucking combine roll up to the cornfield, followed by a dump truck used to cart away the corn. I leapt out of bed and threw on my clothes while Artemis asked, "What is it? What the fuck's *happening*?" I told her for some reason the farmer was harvesting early. I grabbed a hockey bag and ran outside.

By the time I got out there they'd already taken down the first two rows. I waited for them to turn away from me so I could jet across the grassy lot and crash into the cornfield unseen.

Now, when growing pot in cornfields, the most important thing—and I can't emphasize this enough—is to make a fucking *map*. In my rush I'd forgotten to bring my map. Yet

I wasn't that worried since I knew my first four plants were twelve rows in and twenty-four paces over. I pulled them out of the ground and jammed them into the hockey bag.

I finished that patch and headed toward the next, but I didn't realize how much sound is muffled by ten-foot-high corn stalks—suddenly the combine was right on top of me, so close I could see the farmer sitting in his cab. All I could do was crouch down and hope he didn't see me. He passed and I made it to the next planting.

By the time I was done the farmer had cleared the section next to my house. It'd look pretty suspicious if a guy with a hockey bag ran out of the field and into his house, so instead I ran the full length of the field, praying the whole time that the farmer didn't notice his corn stalks were shaking.

When I was fairly sure the farmer was way at the back of the field, I stepped out onto the road and walked home. It looked like I was coming home from early morning hockey practice in the middle of nowhere, except for some reason I'd forgotten to bring a fucking stick.

ONE DAY A young guy named Pat McClutcheon came into the store and introduced himself. He was a clean-cut kid, with short hair and neat clothes, and I had no trouble believing him when he told me he was a chemistry student at the University of Western Ontario. He had an interesting hobby, though: he grew magic mushroom spores.

Soon I was selling his spores in The Organic Traveller, along with how-to guides and mushroom-growing kits. It was even legal: according to the criminal code, psilocybin mushrooms only become "magic" once you picked and dried them. At least, that was our interpretation. It wasn't long before London was flooded with psilocybin spores.

Pat also helped out with my pot supply problem. His family had a cottage in Muskoka, and he said there were lots of deserted islands where you could grow pot completely undetected. My ears perked up.

I'd grown some cannabis up near Orillia the previous year, and had heard of some really successful grows up in that area—the great thing about the Canadian Shield is that there are hardly any trees, so the plants get lots of sunshine and room to grow into the big willowy sativa plants that've always been my favourite. It's also easier to find spots that the douchebag pot hunters won't locate. The only problem is dirt, in that there fucking isn't any. So you have to bring your own.

When planting up in Orillia, I looked for fallen, rotted-out trees. I'd dig out the mushy pulp inside, insert a waterproof bag, punch a few holes for drainage, and then fill it with earth. If you were willing to do all that, you had some of the best outdoor growing conditions you could hope for in a cold country like Canada.

So I liked Pat's idea, even more so since we'd be planting on islands where I figured there wouldn't be any goddamn deer. On the May long weekend we filled Pat's rusty old clanking Subaru with seedlings and dirt and waterproof planting bags and gardening tools. We drove up to his cottage, blasting tunes and smoking spliffs the whole way, and spent the next couple of days boating from one deserted island to the next, planting seedlings and enjoying the sun and the vacation from my responsibilities back in London.

I was excited. The growing conditions looked perfect, and the little islands were all ringed by trees so our plants wouldn't be noticed by passing canoers. The summer went by. I was busy as fuck and hardly thought about the island grows, which is exactly the attitude you should have: the whole reason you're planting outdoors is so you don't have to think about it.

We returned at the end of September. It'd been a hot summer and we weren't as hopeful by now; those islands heat up like big sun-absorbing rocks, which makes sense since that's basically what they are. Sure enough, most of the plants had withered. We managed to harvest nugs from a few plots that'd done well, which was a decent return considering I'd done nothing for them all summer. We loaded up the car with wet cannabis and started back to London, feeling a little bit philosophical. Yes we had some pot, but we could've—or maybe even should've—had a whole lot more.

I was still brooding about what I'd do differently next time when the motor made a sickly wheezing sound and then stopped working. We were lucky to cruise into a gas station/restaurant at the side of the highway. The lot was packed with people leaving from a Neil Young concert at the Barrie amphitheatre. We got out and poked around under the hood, but quickly realized there was fuck all we could do to fix it.

We were just standing there scratching our heads when an OPP car pulled up. The cop rolled down his window. "How you boys doin' today?" he asked.

"We're good. I got a buddy coming from Barrie to get us, plus there's a tow truck on the way."

He nodded. "Make sure you don't stay overnight," he said, and after wishing us a good day he got back in his car and drove away.

Of course, there was no friend, and the last thing we wanted was for a tow truck to haul away a dead car full of nugs.

We knew it was only a matter of time before another cop took an interest, and the next one might be a little more suspicious. So we pushed the car way into the back of the lot, and Pat said he'd figure out what to do with it later.

Then we went from car to car asking for a ride to London. It took forever but we finally found a brother and sister, both of them Western University students who you could tell were clean as fucking whistles. Why they gave us a ride is anybody's guess; maybe Pat being a fellow Western student had something to do with it. We heaved the big bag of weed into the back of their little Honda Civic, and when they asked why we had so much stuff we told them we'd been camping and all our wet gear was in the bag. I even had my fucking *dog* with me—an old Lab-German Shepherd-Great Dane mix named Kootenay after a strain of pot I used to grow called Kootenay Green. He weighed a hundred pounds and looked like a small black bear.

Pat and I rode with the dog stretched over our laps for the two-and-a-half-hour drive back to London. The brother and sister must have known what was in those bags—I mean, they *had* to have smelled it—but they never mentioned it.

Once we made London, we offered them a few joints for their trouble. They politely declined, and I never saw them again.

THE HIPPIE
AND
MR. HEMP

I'D CONTINUED MY photography throughout all this, mostly taking pictures of pot I'd grown or that'd been grown in gardens where I consulted. In the back of the store we had five cabinets we called the Cannabis and Hemp Museum. The first had photos of pot: outdoor gardens, indoor grows, and impressive nugs, some of them taken by other customers and some by me. We called these photos Bud Porn.

The other cabinets held a collection of vintage pipes and bongs, many of them brought in by old hippies; a selection of newspaper and magazine clippings called "Cannabis in the News"; clippings and petitions documenting Chris Clay's constitutional challenge, which went all the way to the Supreme Court of Canada in 2003; and a library of cannabis books that customers could borrow.

One day, a tall guy with long curly black hair and a goatee walked in and looked at my photos. We got to talking, and he told me he really liked my stuff. It turned he was Kyle Kushman, the Cultivation Editor for *High Times* magazine. He lived in Detroit and often drove through Ontario to New York City, where *High Times* was headquartered. The magazine had done a small piece on Hemp Nation's constitutional challenge, so he decided to take a detour through London to check out our weed scene.

As he pored over the photos I could tell by the way he kept raising his eyebrows that he was impressed. "Hey Pete," he said, looking up. "Any chance you'd like to submit some of your photos to the magazine?"

"Sure," I answered, trying to not sound *too* excited. It wasn't easy—I'd been reading *High Times* since I was a teenager, and considered it the bible of cannabis culture.

But it was more than that. I'd gone to fucking *college* for photography. When I became a professional pot crusader I'd had to put my photography dreams on hold, but now it seemed like I could have it both ways. Kyle began running my photos in a section called Grow America, which showcased personal gardens in the US and, now that I was involved, Canada.

Soon he was making regular appearances at the store. Often he showed up with a pair of friends called Big John and Sally. They were good guys, and complete opposites: Big John was businesslike and a little serious, while Sally—short for Salvatore—never had a care in the world. His parents owned a chain of grocery stores in Michigan, and my impression was he only had to work if he *felt* like it.

One thing they had in common was growing pot. We started calling the three of them the Detroit Danksters, and every time they showed up they'd buy a few ounces from me. Soon, they were as big a fans of my weed as they were of my photographs of weed.

Kyle hired me to shoot Big John and Sally's grow in Detroit. As I followed their handwritten directions into town I found myself driving through a scary-ass neighbourhood with crackheads and hard-drug dealers on every corner and police circling above in helicopters. I was *sure* I was fucking lost. But I stuck to the directions, and navigated to a neighbourhood filled with falling down, burnt-out shitholes.

In the middle of it all I found the Danksters' house. It was a modest place with a couple of boarded up windows and a timid Husky looking out the front window. I could feel dozens of pairs of eyes watching me as I unloaded my camera shit. I'd been in a lot of sketchy places but this was the worst by far, and all I could think as I shot their twelve-light basement garden was "man oh man, these guys must have balls the size of watermelons to actually grow cannabis here." They were full of questions since they weren't getting either the potency or the yields that I got in my gardens. I answered as honestly and patiently as I could: I always like an opportunity to generate some karma.

ONE DAY, I was telling Kyle about a new "high-stress training" technique called "super cropping" that I'd been shown by some London growers, and that I'd since used with some success. Basically, you injure the plant by gently crushing the stalk between your thumb and forefinger and then bending it slightly. The plant's natural reaction to the stress is to grow bushier, and sometimes even increase its THC percentage.

It's time consuming as hell, and a bit risky: if you crush the stalk *too* much, you'll compromise the skin and that part of the plant will either die or become too weak to hold any weight. However, if you do it just right, your plant will sprout many more growth shoots to try to heal itself and, as a result, cover itself with gooey smokable nugs. As an added bonus, it puts all of your growth shoots at the same canopy level, so they all bask in full sunlight.

I was a bit of a master at it, so Kyle invited me to the *High Times* Cannabis Cup in Amsterdam to talk about super-cropping, the challenges of growing in a cold environment, and whatever the fuck else I felt like talking about. I went over on *High Times*' dime, the first time I'd been in Europe since my mushroom-funded trip more than a decade earlier. My talk about super-cropping was well-received. I also gave a talk about "flushing," in which I tried to convince a Dutch audience they *had* to stop fertilizing their cannabis during the last couple weeks of the plant's growth cycle.

While I was there, I ran into an old friend named Steve (last names tend not to get used in the cannabis industry), or as we called him, "Breeder Steve"—he was a world-renowned seed cultivator who owned a Vancouver-based seed company called Spice of Life. He told me he was working with a Swiss company called Mr. Hemp, and he introduced me to the owner, whose name (I think) was Peter though of course everyone just called him Mr. Hemp.

It turned out Mr. Hemp was impressed both by my talk on super-cropping, and by the simple fact I was friends with Steve. Right then and there, Mr. Hemp asked me to manage one of his pot fields, which he described as being tucked up in the Swiss Alps near the Italian border. Steve had started the grow with some old Amsterdam genetics he'd acquired through Ed Rosenthal, a famous California cannabis horticulturist who was also known as the "Guru of Ganja"—his Wikipedia page shows a picture of him smoking a joint with Snoop Dogg.

At the time I'd been running the LCS and The Organic Traveller—with all the fucking headaches that went with it—for three years, and a little downtime in the Swiss Alps sounded fantastic. It was a good time for me to go, too: I'd started more gardens in various apartments around London, and production was high enough to meet the demands of the ailing clients coming into the LCS.

I told him I'd do it, and he said he'd be in touch.

The conference ended, and of course I took home dozens of seeds, all bagged and labelled and hidden in my luggage.

SHORTLY AFTER MY return, *High Times* started running my photos as full-page spreads and centrefolds. They also started to send me to photograph gardens throughout Canada.

One of these shoots was set up by an old friend from Vancouver named Kip, though in the cannabis world he was known as Red for his hair colour. He brought me out to meet some dude near Whistler whose name, I think, was Ron—I just called him Mr. Whistler. He was a normal-looking dude with a ponytail, but this guy fucking *owned* Whistler: if you'd bought pot there during that period, there was about a 90 percent chance it'd come through him, and believe me when I say there are a ton of pot smokers in the resort town just north of Vancouver. Whenever he swaggered into a bar there'd be someone there who wanted to buy him a drink just to stay on his good side. Mr. Whistler was king shit in that town and he knew it.

Mr. Whistler was a broker, which is a *huge* business that few people have heard of outside the pot world. Let's say I grow a hundred pounds of weed but don't happen to know a buyer. Enter the broker. You call up a guy like Mr. Whistler, whose business it is to know the sort of people who might buy a few hundred thousand dollars' worth of weed without blinking an eye. In the US alone, brokering is a multi-billion dollar industry, one I dabbled in only briefly. Since it's about money and nothing else, it attracts the sort of people you want nothing to do with: gangsters, sharks, big-time operators, and, if the amounts are big enough, fucking warlords who're slinging dope to fund their armies.

Mr. Whistler knew an old guy called The Hippie who had an outdoor garden somewhere north of Whistler, where he grew a strain of indica called Biker Bob that Mr. Whistler brokered for him. My assignment was to shoot this grow. I flew out to Vancouver, met Red and a few of his friends, and drove north for about an hour and a half along the Sea to Sky Highway. We met up with Mr. Whistler at a pub and drank a pint or two. Then we hit the road again. Mr. Whistler said it was about an hour's drive north-ish on the highway, then another half hour on a logging road.

I told them to let me know when we were close to the turnoff so I could blindfold myself. I planned to stick duct tape inside my sunglasses; anyone we passed would just see a guy wearing sunglasses, as opposed to someone who looked like he was being kidnapped.

Mr. Whistler couldn't believe it. He was all, "Hey man, you're from *High Times*, we trust you, you don't need to do that." So I explained my reasoning. I visited a lot of gardens, and I almost always blindfolded myself, particularly if I didn't know the growers, for a simple reason: if the garden was later raided or robbed, I didn't want to be on the short list of people who knew where it was.

He shrugged and I put the tape on my glasses. I couldn't see shit. For the first little while the ride was more or less smooth, but then we turned onto the logging road and it suddenly got bumpy as shit; when I mentioned it Mr. Whistler was like, "Oh yeah, people get killed along this road all the time." I held the door handle tight so my head didn't hit the roof of the fucking car.

Finally, Mr. Whistler said, "Pete, we've gone far enough, you can take those glasses off."

So I did. To my left was a mountain face. To my right was a cliff, no barrier, the tires knocking gravel into deep fucking space. The lane was barely wide enough for a single vehicle; who knew *what* we'd do if someone came the other way. Just when I was starting to think we'd never get there alive, we turned into a long snaking driveway and came to a cabin in the middle of the bush.

The Hippie was a skinny guy with a long grey beard and a face full of wrinkles who looked about eighty-five. (Apparently he was in his mid-sixties.) He had three pastures of some pretty decent looking sativas, along with the indica garden I'd come to shoot.

I spent a couple hours taking photos, which the magazine later ran in a small spread. They were going to run an article with it but The Hippie said he didn't want his name in any article, which is a pretty common sentiment among old-time growers. They want to live a simple, uncluttered life in the middle of nowhere, just themselves and a cabin and a dog and a field full of pot.

I have to say I understand completely: The Hippie had a nice life cut out for himself in those mountains.

SHORTLY AFTER I returned from BC, Steve called and asked if I still wanted to do some growing in Switzerland. They'd pay me $2,100 a week, I'd have two people working for me, and I could take away as much pot as I could carry come harvest time.

I thought for a few seconds about whether it was a good time to go. I had a really good employee at The Organic Traveller who everyone called Bong Boy, though after the longest time I learned he was named Chris. Bong Boy was a skinny kid with a red mohawk, one of the original crew who hung around Hemp Nation. He was known for trying to start an event called The Bong Olympics, in which people would compete to do the biggest bong hit, to hold in a bong hit the longest, to build the best bong. While I don't think it ever actually happened, they sure had a shitload of fun practicing.

Bong Boy's grandmother had left him enough of an inheritance that he didn't care about getting paid. For a long time he volunteered at Hemp Nation and then The Organic Traveller, though now that Organic was more stable I figured the time had come to start paying him. Soon after, he took on more and more responsibility until he was pretty much running the store.

I'd also taken on a staffer at the LCS named Rob Newman. Along with his husband Danny, Rob had been one of the earliest members of the society; like a lot of HIV-positive patients, he found cannabis stimulated his appetite and prevented wasting syndrome, a common effect of HIV infection. I also knew him from when he'd worked at the AIDS Committee of London, which had an office above Hemp Nation. After he'd volunteered with the LCS for a while I hired him as a manager. He did such a good job that I knew the society would be in good hands if I left for the summer.

Finally, I knew that Artemis would be around to help both Bong Boy at the shop and Rob at the centre. She also told me she'd take care of my dog.

"So," Mr. Hemp asked. "You comin'?"

"Sure," I said, and fucked off to Switzerland.

LOVE THE ONE YOU'RE WITH

FROM ZURICH I TOOK a train to Lugano and met Steve and his pregnant wife, Kristy. I dropped my bags at Steve's flat and we went to meet the owner of the land the pot field was planted on, a little Italian guy named Titsiano—or TeeTee—who didn't speak a word of English. Apparently he spoke such a weird Swiss-Italian dialect that even some of his best friends from his village could barely understand him. He'd also trained for a year in the Swiss Army and had a nice collection of guns. This wasn't unusual for Swiss men—military service was compulsory—but the way he used his guns *was* a bit different: he used to smoke weed through the barrels, just like Willem Dafoe's character in *Platoon*.

The next day we picked up another guy, Barge, a photographer from a Vancouver magazine called *Cannabis*

Culture who was travelling around Europe taking pictures of pot, and then we all headed to the field. As we climbed higher and higher into the mountains, I grew more and more excited thinking about the great big willowy sativas I could grow in all that fresh air.

On the way, Steve told me he had some bad news. There'd been a guy working in the field from Detroit named Donnie. He and his daughter, Anna, were the two assistants Mr. Hemp had promised me. A few days earlier, some agents from the immigration department showed up to check his paperwork—but Donnie didn't have a work permit or a return ticket, and was wanted for drug offences back in the US. He asked the agents for a few minutes to look for his nonexistent paperwork and, when the agents' backs were turned, he literally ran down the other side of the mountain. (I ran into him at the airport in Zurich on my way home later; he apologized for leaving me short-handed, and gave me a nice chunk of hash to smuggle home.)

The field was 2,400 square metres at an altitude of 2,400 metres, on a beautiful plateau surrounded by mountain peaks, all within eyeshot of the Italian border. The plants were about waist-high and still vegetating when I arrived. They left me there with a bottle of Bailey's, a bag of groceries, and an army tent. Barge and I spent the night smoking hash and freaking out about all the animal sounds echoing through the mountains—they sounded like fucking *people*, signaling to one another.

The next morning, Steve showed up and we talked about the grow. I asked him what kind of irrigation system

Mr. Hemp had installed. "Well," he said, "there are reservoirs over there and over there, and we keep the watering cans over there..."

"You mean you expect me to hand-water a field this size?"

"Yeah," he said. "Plus, there's something else you should know."

A short time before I'd arrived, Mr. Hemp had been arrested for selling pot online to a minor. The project's financial backer had bailed, so I wouldn't be getting the weekly salary I'd been promised. Steve told me not to worry; once we grew the pot we'd sell it ourselves and I'd make more in the long run. But in the meantime, I'd be all alone, no heat or electricity or helpers, taking a huge field of weed to harvest.

"I'd understand if you want me to take you to the airport," Steve said.

I looked at the field. There were hundreds and hundreds of plants, all of them waist-high and healthy. The sun was bright, the sky a solid blue. There was a light, cooling breeze.

"Fuck it," I told him. "I'm in."

I TACKED TOGETHER a lean-to, and had them bring me a table and chair, and a candle for reading at night. I hauled water and pruned the plants and cooked over open fires.

A big part of my job was keeping people away, which was a constant problem—Switzerland has a trans-country hiking trail that passed right by the field. So I was always walking out to meet nosy hikers. Most of them spoke

German, sometimes French or Italian or Swiss, but it could've been fucking martian for all I knew: it all sounded the same to me. The one word I did learn was *hanf*, which is German for hemp—I'd point to the field and say, "Hanf! Hanf!" and their faces would light up and they'd be all like, "Ah-ha! Marijuana!" and I'd be, "no, no, it's hanf! For clothes! You know... to make clothes!"

When TeeTee and Steve had originally planted the field, it was in the middle of fucking *no*where. Now there was a market being built half a kilometre down the road, and the once-lonely road was filled with workers, all blowing dust on my field as they drove by. And the drivers would notice the field, and I'd be out there again, pointing stupidly, saying, "Hanf! Hanf! For clothes!"

It was worse at night. Since I was surrounded by mountain roads I could see the headlights of cars coming for miles. Most of them would continue on to the next village, but sometimes their headlights would go dark and I just fucking *knew* they were out there trying to see what they could get.

When I started the job, TeeTee tried to give me a shotgun filled with rock salt that I could fire at anyone trying to steal the plants. I told him I didn't do guns, and the last thing I needed was for the police to catch me, a *foreigner*, in the middle of a pot field with a weapon. "So, no," I told him. "If anyone shows up to rob the field, I'll do whatever I can to stop them. But if they have a gun, I'll fucking help them load it into their truck. Do we understand each other?"

Instead, I got myself a six-foot-long stick, and a two-foot club I called King Cannabis after Red carved a face in it one night. If people got too nosy I'd show up, club in hand, asking if I could help them. Mostly this worked.

But one night, TeeTee showed up with a complete stranger, some friend of his I guessed, though I couldn't understand their language so who the fuck knew. We hung out near the fire I lit every night. I just *knew* this guy was playing TeeTee, who was probably trying to impress him with his big field of pot.

I went on my nightly walkabout. When I hit the field, I heard this dude let out a huge roar, and then I heard rustling along the fence line.

Sure enough, the next morning a bunch of plants were missing from that corner of the field: the so-called friend must've had some friends with him who robbed us when we were up near the fire. Steve swore he was going to find the guy and kill him, though of course he never did since the robber had enough sense to completely fucking disappear.

Steve was also calmed by the fact that it wasn't that big a loss: including the theft, we figured we might lose 5 percent of the whole crop, which was a fuckload better than the 50 to 90 percent you could count on losing from an outdoor grow in Ontario.

I FINALLY GOT some help about six-and-a-half weeks in when Steve brought in three guys to help with the end-of-season trimming. One of them was Red. There was a guy from Washington State we called Smiley, in the same way you call a bald guy Curly—he was miserable as fuck and didn't last long before disappearing for good. The other guy was named Jimmy, though I called him Yimmit; he was the complete opposite of Smiley, always in good spirits and willing to get shit done. Sometimes, Breeder Steve would come by and offer to help, which to him meant taking a nap in a hammock overlooking the field.

So it was mostly Red and me working away in the fields. One day, out of the blue, Anna, the daughter of Detroit Donnie, finally showed up and helped with the trimming. She and I soon got pretty friendly, which was fine with Artemis; we were both firm believers in the "love the one you're with" mentality and had a bit of an open relationship, particularly when one of us was away. Anna stayed for a couple of weeks and then one morning she was gone, just like that.

We harvested the weed and divided it up between TeeTee and Steve. We didn't have a place to properly dry it so we took it back to Steve's flat and laid it on his terracotta floor. Then we rented a U-Haul truck, filled it to the roof with pot, and drove to a warehouse that TeeTee rented. Steven sold some of his weed and gave me the money he owed me. As a bonus, he gave me a few kilos that I was free to sell up in Zurich.

WHEN WE HAD something to show for our efforts, a bunch of seed bank owners from Holland descended on Steve's apartment in Lugano—there was Arjan from a company called Green House Seeds, Luke from Paradise Seeds, and Henke from Dutch Passion. We were growing some interesting new strains and they were curious to see what we'd take to that year's Cannabis Cup in Amsterdam.

I was proud of two strains in particular. The first was an incredibly powerful indica I called Ortega. The second was a light, flavourful sativa I called Fast Spear. Of course, they all loved the Ortega—there's a lot of macho bullshit in the pot world, and guys always prefer the strongest pot, if only to show they can handle it. I preferred the flavour and light, uplifting buzz I got from Fast Spear. We argued and argued about which pot to enter into the cup, and finally we decided that Steve would enter the Ortega under the Spice of Life banner, and I'd try my luck with Fast Spear.

The next week I flew to Amsterdam carrying just over a kilo of Fast Spear, as well as half a pound of hash and all our other entries for that year's Cannabis Cup. I had it vacuum packed and carefully stuffed into my backpack.

Now you'd think if security were going to search anyone in the Zurich airport it would be me: I'd just spent three months living in a fucking pot field, my clothes were hemp and hippie as shit, and I had my new dreadlocks shoved up into a tam. Last but not least, I had the King Cannabis club I'd used to ward off pot hunters—by then I considered it a good-luck charm—tied to the outside of my pack. Still, I got on the plane.

I showed up at the Amsterdam airport all smiles, believing that if you don't act like a criminal they won't treat you like one. When I got to customs I had a look around. I watched how the custom agents were screening people entering their areas, and I noticed that none of the agents could actually see one another.

I struck up a conversation with a snowboarder standing next to me so it'd look like we were travelling together.

When it was my turn, I noticed that Agent A was looking at me, so I started speaking to Agent B, who was actually searching another traveller. This meant that Agent A thought that Agent B was dealing with me, and Agent B thought I belonged to Agent A.

I strolled right through customs, whistling that old Arlo Guthrie song about drug smuggling: *Comin' into Los Angeles / Bringin' in a couple of keys / Don't touch my bags if you please, mister customs man...*

SO—THE CANNABIS CUP. The world's biggest and most important pot competition. My strategy was simple: the theme of that year's cup was "Honour the Goddess," and all the judges were going to be women. I knew that most women don't like getting so stoned they can barely move. Women like getting all giggly and energetic, they like something that'll keep them on the dance floor. Women like getting high, not stoned.

Women, I knew, like the beautiful and sexy sativa.

I got comfortable at our booth, which bore the name of Steve and Kip's company, "Legend Seed Co." I went on a charm offensive. Every chance I got, I flirted with the judges and played up the romance of Fast Spear—how I'd spent three months living in a pot field to grow it, how it was made with all organic products, how I'd smuggled it into Amsterdam in a backpack.

A Brazilian woman named Josette was in the booth beside me promoting an early generation vaporizer. She agreed to let me supply her booth with our products so that people could try her vaporizers: I got my product out there, and every time someone tried it I was right there to tell them about the pot and how good it was to party on.

After a week of hard partying it was time for the judging. Ortega didn't place, and Fast Spear won bronze.

The next day I flew back to Canada not a penny richer than when I left, since I'd spent every dime I made in Switzerland in a single week in Amsterdam. I did have one thing going for me, though.

I was now the guy who'd bred the third best sativa on earth.

SEEING
GREEN

I ARRIVED HOME in the spring of 2001, happy to find both my businesses still running smoothly. The Organic Traveller, which I'd left with Bong Boy, was making just as much money as before I'd left. And the London Compassion Society was now operating out of a storage area behind The Organic Traveller—Rob and Artemis had cleared out the massive amount of shit back there and cleaned up the space, a task I'd intended to do before leaving for Switzerland.

So I was pleased for two reasons. The first was that the move had fucking got *done*. The second was that Rob and Artemis had found an old collection of pot I'd stashed there and forgotten about, thirty or forty jars all labelled with each strain, when I had grown it, and the type of fertilizer I'd used. Of course, the pot itself was all brown and beige—the chlorophyll leaks out if you don't put it in a freezer—but that wasn't the point. I'd worked hard to collect every strain I'd ever grown, and finding those lost jars made me feel like my collection was a little more complete.

We ran the LCS out of that back room for a couple of months. More and more clients signed up and it soon became obvious that we needed more space. I was beginning to envision the LCS as more of a holistic treatment centre, where sick people could come to receive therapy that had nothing to do with cannabis.

That wish became a reality a few months later. The law office across the street moved out and their beautiful storefront became available: wood floors, sixteen-foot-high arched windows, a kitchen, a reception area, and lots of lots of space. But the best thing? It had once been used as a bank, so it came with an actual fucking *vault* we could keep our weed in.

I was already renting a space for The Organic Traveller in the same building, so I contacted the property manager, who turned out to be the vice-president of a large, London-based property management firm called Farhi Holdings. (To this day, if you drive through London or St. Thomas you'll see the name Farhi on "For Lease" signs everywhere.) His name was Muky, a small, bald Israeli guy who was extremely tough and extremely fair. We got along, and it turned out he was pro-cannabis. He named a high price, I named a low price, and we met in the middle.

The London Compassion Society moved into a 1,400-square-foot space in an elegant new building on Richmond Street, right in the heart of London's business area. We hired an LCS member named Albert to be our cleaner, and we hired Sarah Delaney, the young woman who was arrested when Hemp Nation was raided the second time, as a receptionist. Rob and I both had offices, and there was a kitchen where our security guy, a massive tattooed biker named Marcel, liked to bake cookies. And we had a vault full of weed.

In short order, we brought in three or four therapists offering massage therapy, shiatsu, aromatherapy and craniosacral treatments. We had a yoga instructor, Steve, a huge guy with full-sleeve tattoos who was also an LCS client. On top of regular yoga classes, he offered after-hours nude yoga for gay men. (We learned not to ask too much about what went on in the yoga studio when one of the staff walked in during a "downward dog" pose.) For the first time, the LCS had a revenue stream other than cannabis sales.

We also had a room we called our "safe inhalation site." When we had been neighbours with the AIDS Committee of London they were sharing quarters with Counterpoint, London's needle exchange program. Counterpoint also offered safe injection sites. It occurred to me that maybe the pot smokers of London could benefit from a similar concept. Maybe they were young and weren't allowed to smoke at home. Maybe they were homeless and didn't want to risk getting busted by smoking on the street. Maybe they were worried about the health consequences of smoking joints and wanted to try our massive, $600 Volcano vaporizer. Maybe they were new medical clients, and needed someone to show them the different ways you can smoke cannabis. Or maybe they just wanted some company. Whatever the reason, people were now welcome to smoke in our inhalation site for free, and believe me when I say they came in fucking droves.

Still, I had my usual problem: with five hundred registered users, and more signing on every day, we needed a shitload of weed. This has been a theme of my life. I've always grown a shitload of pot because, as a supplier to the underground compassion movement, I fucking *needed* a lot of pot.

Apart from the Hill Street garden I didn't have time to do much growing. I did, however, do a lot of consulting. Aspiring growers would come to me and I'd advise them on strains, tell them what equipment they needed, and show them what they needed to do. In return, they sold a certain amount of their yield to the LCS at reduced prices, so that I could then turn around and pass those savings on to my clients.

When apartments opened up above us, I rented them and sublet them to growers for the same deal I always offered: I'd pay a portion of their rent in return for a percentage of their harvest. If I also set them up with equipment, that upped the amount of pot they had to give me. I had custom deals with each grower, some of whom had tiny two-light ops in closets, while others had huge twelve-light basement grows.

Of course, all of this was going on right under the noses of the London police department: I had a commercial space in the heart of London, I had growers all over the city, and my principle activity was doling out an illegal drug. Yes, it was brazen. Yes, it was a risk. But we always treated the police respectfully, and in return they were fair with us.

Plus, the police knew that if they did arrest me I'd fight them with everything I had—and the LCS had *way* more resources than Chris Clay had when Hemp Nation got busted. There was also the compassion aspect: I was selling to people who, in many cases, were desperately ill. The police must've *known* how it would look if those people took the stand and testified that my product was the only thing that gave them any relief.

WITH THE LCS established in its new space and everything running smoothly, I decided it was a good time for one of my regular hiatuses from smoking pot. My rule was I had to quit for at least thirty days. I could do longer if I wanted—and I often did—but I found I needed at least thirty days to completely clear my head and take stock.

I'd done this about once a year since I was thirteen, though my reasons for doing so were always different. When I was thirteen and had just failed every single class, including fucking *gym*, I was like, "Oh man, I am fucking up my *life*, I gotta get my shit together for a bit." When I got a little bit older, I wanted to give my lungs a break. There was no vaping back then and I exposed myself to a lot of unfiltered smoke. I'm all about respecting the body. When I was a bit older still, I found I wanted to give my brain a break once a year, to step outside the cloud and see what was actually out there.

In my mid-twenties, when I first took over The Organic Traveller, I quit smoking pot to set an example for the stoner kids who were always coming into the shop. A lot of them smoked all day every day, and it was affecting their lives: like any drug, pot can and will have negative consequences if you use too much. These kids would be like, "Fuck parents, fuck teachers, I'm doing shitty in school, my guidance counsellor smelled weed on me and now I'm in big trouble..." I really enjoyed talking with these kids about the problems they had at home or at school or with their parents or whatever. For a while I even considered getting into adolescent psychology as a career.

They wouldn't listen to anyone else, but they'd listen to me, the guy with the dreadlocks behind the counter. I'd try to convince them it was cool to be different from your friends and say "no thanks" once in a while. If nothing else, I'd remind them that if they quit smoking pot for a month, when they started again they'd have no tolerance and they'd get twice as fucking high on half as much.

Once, when I was about twenty, I quit smoking for a full eighteen months. Then one night I was sitting around with some friends in New York who were all doing bong hits—I remember Toast was there—and I was like, Fuck it, I've gone a year and a half, I'm gonna have a bong hit or two. Instead I had five or six and immediately knew I'd had too much. You know how it is: the mind explodes, the nausea sets in.

I staggered into the bathroom to splash some water on my face. Maybe it was the lighting or maybe it was me freaking out, but when I looked in the mirror I looked totally fucking *green*. After a few minutes, a buddy from across the street named Steve walked by the bathroom and noticed me staring at my reflection. "Dude," he said, "are you okay? You look kinda green."

I became convinced that somehow the chlorophyll from the plant had entered my system, and was physically turning me a different colour. Never underestimate what you can convince yourself of when you're that fucked up.

Things only got worse. When I used to deliver meat for Hungry Howie's, I had to make notes of who got what and when, and I found I could save a lot of time if I made those notes while driving to my next delivery. Eventually I was able to write notes without actually looking at the paper. But then I started to notice this fucked-up behaviour: if I smoked pot, the next morning I'd wake up and find little handwritten notes next to my bed, just like I used to write when I delivered meat. Instead of sleepwalking, I was fucking sleep*writing*, which was freaky enough I started to think, I dunno, maybe I should add a few more months to this hiatus...

POT AFFECTS DIFFERENT people in different ways, and I was starting to realize I'd developed a neural circuitry that, at times, couldn't tolerate the drug. For one thing, I couldn't turn my brain off and had trouble sleeping when I was high. I also found it suppressed my appetite and enhanced my aches and pains, whereas most people I knew said it did the opposite.

The year the LCS moved into our new offices on Richmond Street, I went a little further. As well as pot, I also quit alcohol, cigarettes, caffeine, and sex. It wasn't like I was doing a Buddhist enlightenment thing; I actually had a separate reason for quitting them all.

A friend told me there was no way I could quit smoking cigarettes, so I gave them up just to show him I could.

I had noticed I couldn't get going in the morning until I had my caffeine, and I can't stand being dependent on any substance, so I quit coffee.

With all the stress of running the shop and the LCS—I worked twelve hours a day, minimum—I'd noticed a small uptick in my booze consumption whenever I stopped smoking pot, so I quit that as well.

As for sex, I'd fallen for a new woman, Andrea (I called her Dr. Dre since she was working on a doctorate in environmental science). She wanted us to quit having sex for a few months before we started having sex with each other. So I figured what the fuck, I'll give that a go as well.

I lived like a fucking monk for a month. I'd just turned thirty. When the month of not smoking pot was over I decided to do another month. I never started smoking again.

As I write this, I've only touched cannabis once in the past seventeen years, and even that was an accident: Sarah, our receptionist at the LCS, brought in a bunch of pot cookies. Somehow, she totally spaced on the fact I hadn't used cannabis for years, and offered me one (which sounds pretty irresponsible, I know, but when you're in the compassion business there's always weed around). I didn't know the cookies were laced. I took one into my office and by the time she came running in to warn me, it was too late.

I spent the next few hours sitting in the corner of my office, just fucking *vibrating*, and convinced I'd made the right decision to stop consuming cannabis.

In other words, I was completely cannabis-free, and had nothing to blame but myself for the decision I made next.

GROW WEST, YOUNG MAN

DURING SOME OF my trips out west, I'd got to know a guy that everyone called Blue, a nickname he'd picked up since he'd spent about a decade following the Dead in a vehicle he called his Blue Disco Van. (Also, his best friend was Red, so...) I got on with Blue immediately. I liked his energy, his knee-length dreads, his hippie girlfriend.

Blue was a very successful pot broker—he made money like it was going out of style. He also dabbled in the restaurant business and had a taste for good wine; he once took his father out for a birthday dinner and had the restaurant special-order a bottle from his dad's birth year.

In the spring of 2003, I got a call from Blue. He told me he knew a guy with a grow in the BC interior who was getting super shitty yields and wanted to get more into greenhouse growing. Blue asked if I'd be interested in moving out there to help this guy with his next crop. In exchange for a season's work, he said I'd get a quarter of the garden, meaning I'd stand to earn about $100,000. Even though Switzerland had been a bit rough, I was immediately interested.

The money had nothing to do with it—again, if you're only thinking about money you'll grow shitty pot. I was ready for a new adventure. I knew I could trust Bong Boy with The Organic Traveller, and Rob Newman with the London Compassion Society, and I figured this'd be a good opportunity to learn about greenhouse grows.

Blue had also promised that we'd only grow organically, and that a portion of the grow would be sold at a reduced price to the British Columbia Compassion Club Society, which was run by an amazing woman named Hilary Black.

Hilary used to work at Hemp BC, a store owned by well-known pot activist Marc Emery, who I've always called the Dark Enemy. He's one of those fuckwads who exist in the pot world—let's just say I mistrust his motives and leave it at that.

By now Hilary was a part of the compassion movement, and became such a leader that I labelled her the Queen of Compassion. She was excited when I told her I'd be able to send some organically grown BC Bud her way.

Finally, I'd always thought that maybe one day I'd permanently relocate to British Columbia, to enjoy the scenery and the thriving cannabis culture. This seemed like a good opportunity to check it out.

"Sure," I told him, "why not?"

BY THE END of that week, I'd spent every cent of my savings on a 1995 Jeep Cherokee Sport that was the size and shape of a small Hummer. I drove out in April of 2002. I'd never crossed Canada by land, and was curious to see what the prairies looked like. Plus, it'd mean I wouldn't have to find a vehicle once I got out there.

I also bought a trailer, in which I put all my cannabis photos from over the years (I figured I'd use my downtime out west to sort through them all) and a 1966 Wurlitzer jukebox that belonged to my ex-girlfriend Artemis. She was now living in Vancouver, and I agreed I'd haul it out for her.

Right from the start the trip was a complete fucking disaster. The night before I left, Kootenay was sprayed in the face by a skunk, meaning I had to share the truck with a dog who reeked.

Near Parry Sound, I drove into a valley during a sudden snow storm, and the road was so slippery the truck couldn't make it out of the valley. All I could do was pull over, sleep in the Jeep with my stink-ass dog, and wait for the conditions to clear.

My trailer hitch was nearly ripped off near Sudbury, so I had to waste another day getting it repaired by some Slayer-loving grease monkey on the outskirts of town. As soon as I left Sudbury I hit another blizzard that quickly turned to whiteout conditions; again, all I could do was pull over and wait for conditions to clear. I made it as far as Winnipeg before my transmission blew. Luckily I had friends there who put me up for a few nights while a new one got installed.

The bad weather continued into BC, and the Jeep had all kinds of trouble hauling a fucking jukebox up and down the slick mountains. All in all, it took eight fucking days to get out there. By the time I arrived, I was already starting to think maybe I should've thought this whole thing over a bit more.

FINALLY I DROVE down a steep, rocky path into a forested valley and arrived at the farm, near the tiny North Thompson Valley town of Little Fort. This is where I first shook hands with Jay, the guy who needed help with his cannabis operation. He was my age, more or less, with short hair. Apparently he worked in film production before switching to pot growing. He had a couple of successful grows under his belt, and it gave him a cockiness he didn't, in any way, deserve. Right off, I pegged him as the kind of guy who was in the pot business for all the wrong reasons.

Though Jay lived in a beautiful log house, I was going to be staying in a tiny off-the-grid cabin with an outhouse. This was part of the agreement, and didn't bother me: I'd lived that way in Switzerland. Every once in a while I like to give up all the shit that Westerners take for granted. I guess it's my thing about dependency: I like knowing I can not only do without, but be happy about it.

The first thing Jay did was show me the section of forest where he wanted to put the greenhouse, and the whole time I was thinking, Wait a minute, Blue told me the greenhouse was already fucking *built*. I told Jay I was hired to grow pot, not do construction, and as long as he was clear on that I was happy to help him design the thing. So that's what we did. I worked on the design and he hired a few labourers to put the thing together. When it was built we moved in a bunch of clones we'd grown inside an old chicken coop.

Almost immediately, Jay and I started to butt heads over who was going to buy the pot. I understood that we'd sell it—or at least a big chunk of it—to Hilary Black of the BC Compassion Club Society in Vancouver. But Jay said no, Blue had found a big buyer in the US who had pledged to buy every pound we grew at top dollar.

I explained to Jay that wasn't how I worked, that if a portion of my weed didn't go for compassion purposes, then I did not grow weed. Period.

"Fuck, man," he said. "Those compassion people don't *pay* as much."

I proposed a compromise. All of the greenhouse grow would go to Blue's buyer in the states, and I'd plant another garden outside and grow some weed that I'd sell to the BCCCS. Jay agreed, and I found a patch of land at the bottom of a stream-fed ravine and planted a bunch of clones.

For a while, everything was okay. I worked during the day in the greenhouse, and after hours I'd walk down to the outdoor grow and do all the trimming and fertilizing. The greenhouse plants were doing well, even though Jay insisted on using cheap, synthetic fertilizer. My outdoor plants also started shooting up, and I could tell I was going to get a pretty decent crop for Hilary.

Then, Jay told me one afternoon that he had a situation: the guys in the US wanted more than we'd produce in the greenhouse. He paused, and then said he "had no choice" but to sell the US buyers my outdoor plants as well.

I was furious.

"Look, Pete, it's *my* garden," he said.

All I could do was shake my head and say, "No, man, it's *our* garden."

The ravine grow *was* on Jay's property, and Jay was one of those douchebags who always think, What's mine is mine, and that I worked for fucking *him*—the fact that pot grows better when people work communally would never enter his pin-sized head.

Of course it didn't matter. Nothing but *nothing* was going to change the fact that Jay was taking my outdoor weed, and if I didn't like it, fine, I could just leave.

Again, I came up with a compromise. I'd scouted out a plot of land on top of the small mountain behind Jay's house, a spot where any clones with a bit of sativa in them would feel right at home. Even better, it was outside of Jay's property, so he couldn't lay claim to them. I told him I was going to start a compassion grow up there, and the least he could do was help me haul some dirt to the top of the mountain.

Things were fine again for the next little while. Well, not *fine*, exactly, but at least things were working: during the day I cared for the gardens in the greenhouse and the ravine, and after hours I'd ride my bike up a little dirt path to my mountaintop grow.

The plants in the greenhouse started to flower. Unfortunately, it was hot as shit in that greenhouse; during the vegetative period I'd tried different ways to ventilate, with limited success. As soon as the flowers opened they started to melt, which caused a lot of mildew (or, as I liked to call it, "bud rot").

There are organic ways to deal with this: you prune more rigorously, you install more ventilation, and you cull some of the plants so the rest can breathe better. Naturally, since they were expensive and time-consuming, Jay would have nothing to do with these solutions. Instead, he

insisted on treating them with all kinds of fucking pesti-
cides, herbicides, and fungicides. When I protested, he said
they were *his* plants and they were in *his* greenhouse, and
I was like, Well then why the fuck did you hire an organic
farmer to help you out?

He even insisted on burning sulphur, which is a way of
fighting bud rot in its early stages. When sprayed too late—
as it would be here—it affects the smell and flavour of the
weed. If you've ever smoked pot that's been treated to a
sulphur burn you know what I'm talking about. You can
fucking *taste* it on the tip of your tongue.

Again, I complained: "You're gonna grow shitty tasting
pot."

He was like, "Who cares, as long as it gets you stoned—
besides, I've got a buyer lined up and do you really think
they care?"

That's when it hit me.

I was doing everything I'd always promised myself I'd
never do. I was growing shitty, nonorganic pot, and I was
doing it strictly for profit. I'd gone to the dark side. When
you do that, things always, *always* start to fuck up. It's
Karma 101. The universe senses what you're doing, and
figures you need your ass kicked.

I'D BROUGHT A longboard with me from Ontario. When I
was scouting out my mountaintop grow I discovered a steep
paved logging road near the farm, and one day I got the
bright idea to ride down it. I had three or four runs under
my belt when I severely fucking crashed. I ended up in
the hospital in the nearby town of Clearwater, where they

told me I'd fractured my L5 vertebra. Luckily, it was minor enough that they didn't put me in traction, but for the rest of my time in BC it hurt whenever I moved too quickly.

Then, my mountaintop grow started failing. I wasn't surprised; I'd put the plants in way too late. Also, I'd had to use cuttings from the greenhouse grow, which weren't necessarily varieties designed for the top of a mountain. And since I was taking care of the two gardens on Jay's property, as those plants started to bloom and needed more attention I was getting off work later and later. Since my back hurt so fucking much it took me forever to get to the mountaintop, so I often got up there too late to get much done before I had to ride my bike back down in failing light.

One night, I pushed it a little too much: by the time I was done it was pitch-black. I couldn't find my fucking bike. I searched and searched, or at least I searched as much as I could without getting lost in all that darkness, until I finally realized I'd have to come back up and look for it in daylight. So I started walking down the little switchback road to Jay's property.

That's when I heard it, above me on the side of the mountain: *movement*. I stopped, and the noise stopped. I started walking, and the noise started again. I stopped again and the noise stopped again and that's when I knew I was being tracked.

I always carried bear spray with me, but I knew that bears are noisy motherfuckers that crash clumsily through the woods, so whatever was tracking me wasn't a bear. This was most likely a cougar. I knew they were around since they were always sneaking onto Jay's property and eating out of the dogs' food bowls. The cat was high above, making me look a lot smaller and more worthy of being prey. If I'd made the mistake of breaking into a run I'm pretty sure it would've attacked, but I made it home, scared shitless the entire way.

So now, I was nervous about going up to my mountain-top grow after work, only I *had* to tend to those plants at night since I was so busy during the day. Slowly, I felt my compassion garden—my only real reason for wanting to be there—slipping through my fingertips.

ONE DAY I drove to Kamloops to buy fertilizer. At the sup-ply depot, I stepped on a rusty nail while carrying a fifty-pound bag of Pro-Mix. The nail went through the sole of my Birkenstock and almost completely through my foot. I had to go back to Emergency, where they bandaged it up, gave me a tetanus shot, and warned me to keep it clean, which I did by dousing it with hydrogen peroxide—not the 3 percent solution that most people keep in their medicine cabinets, but the industrial strength, 35 percent stuff that I used in my homemade fertilizer profile. Now my foot, as well as my back, hurt like hell.

Shortly after my accident with the nail, I drove to a town called Hope, about two-thirds of the way from Jay's property to Vancouver. I had some friends there, and whenever I had some time off I'd drive down with my dog Kootenay, crash on their sofa, get a little R & R, and try to decompress.

This time, Kootenay got into a fight with my buddy's dog. I can't imagine what set it off, seeing as they were both peaceful animals, but all of a sudden they were snarling and barking and biting each other, so I ran in and hauled off Kootenay and that's when the other dog chomped down on my left foot. He really got me too: my fucking tendon was hanging out, blood was everywhere. And the worst part was that the dog was a Golden Retriever. I mean, who the *fuck* gets bit by a Golden Retriever?

I went to Emergency, *again*, and they bandaged me up and told me to keep it clean and elevated. They offered to give me a tetanus shot but I told them I'd had one just a few weeks earlier. The next day, I drove back to Jay's. It was a two-and-a-half-hour drive along the Coquihalla Highway, which is one of the most dangerous highway stretches in Canada. By the time I got back, my sneaker was full of blood.

So now I had a fucked up back and a torn-up foot, all so I could help my scumbag boss sell tainted fucking pot to some gangsters in the US.

I did have one thing to lift my spirits, however. Dr. Dre was going to come out and stay with me for a month or two before flying back east when school resumed in September. I was really into her, and given all the bullshit that'd happened I was looking forward to her visit so much that I decided to make a huge gesture for her.

She loved to eat meat and fish, so long as the animal had been ethically raised. I hadn't eaten fish since I was super young—growing up on the beach, fish always smelled to me like low tide, and I never really liked it—but during my stay out west I'd learned to fly fish.

A grower I knew named Jimmy lived in a small town a couple hours away called Falkland. Jimmy also had a greenhouse grow, and he gave me a lot of advice for the one I was operating. He was an avid fly fisher; there are undeveloped freshwater lakes all through BC's interior that fishers just love. So he showed me how to tie my own flies, and I'd go fishing with him—which meant getting up at four in the fucking morning.

Still, I didn't eat any of the fish I could now catch—or at least I didn't until Dre confirmed she was coming out. Just to show her how game I was, I went out in a canoe and caught a beautiful twelve-inch rainbow trout. That night, I showed my catch to Jay and Blue and his girlfriend, and they were super excited: in all the time they'd been there no one had caught a fish that big in that lake. I wanted to prepare it myself, so Blue showed me how to gut and clean it—which was disgusting—and they took pictures, which I sent to Dre to show her how excited I was that she was coming.

We cooked it with garlic and butter, half on the stovetop and half on an open fire, and they were all like, Oh man this is the best fish I've ever tasted. Meanwhile I was working hard just to choke the fucking thing down.

A few days later, I got a note from her saying that she'd met another dude *on the way out to BC*, she'd totally fallen in love with him, and she wasn't coming out anymore.

I was driving along a mountain road after reading her letter when I suddenly had the impulse to turn the wheel and drive off the fucking cliff. I might've done it if I hadn't had Kootenay in the car with me. Instead, I turned around and headed back to Jay's.

When I got there, Blue came running up to me, looking all worked up. That's when he told me his contact in the US fell through. It seemed they had some concerns about smuggling the weed over the border, and had found a hookup in California that would be a lot cheaper since they wouldn't need any mules to take it over a border.

It was weird, though: he was all smiles. I asked him why. "Pete," he said, "don't you get it? Now we can sell it all to Hilary at the BCCCS. It's what you wanted all along."

"No fucking way. Jay sprayed that weed with all kinds of poison and he fed it all kinds of shit, and then he sulphur-burned the *shit* out of it. There's no way I'm selling it to the BCCCS. I wouldn't put my reputation on the line like that, and neither are *you* since I'm gonna tell Hilary not to buy that shit. I mean, you can't expect people with compromised immune systems to smoke that shit, it's liable to make them even worse. So fuck you guys, I'm not doing it and neither are you and you're going to have to find someone else to buy the fucking weed."

A few days after *that*, a nearby town called McLure caught fire and it soon spread to the woods around us.

CAMPFIRE WEED

LATER, I HEARD the fire started when some stupid fucker having a smoke out back of the only restaurant in town flipped his butt into some wild grass. It hadn't rained forever so the grass went up and the wind carried the flames from there.

From Jay's property we could see thick columns of smoke rise up from the town. It quickly spread. Though at first it looked like the fire was going to miss us, it still raged close enough to us that our eyes were burning and we were coughing from the smoke. We had just started harvesting, though with all the fucking smoke in the air we couldn't see fifteen feet in front of our faces. It was impossible to work on the farm, so we took some of the weed to a friend of Jay's about forty minutes away, well out of the fire zone, to trim and cure it.

There we discovered we had yet another major fuck-up on our hands: the smoke had infected the harvest. The weed smelled and tasted like a fucking campfire. We started calling it "campfire weed," and we knew that even if we *did* manage to find anyone stupid enough to buy it we'd get pennies on the dollar.

The winds shifted and the fire turned straight toward Jay's property. All the local radio and TV stations issued evacuation orders, which we didn't get since we were in a valley and the air was full of smoke and reception was shitty. We only heard we had to leave when the neighbour, a grizzly old-timer named Eddie who grew a little pot of his own, came over and said, "You guys know you got to get the fuck out, right?"

Jay packed up his wife and his two-year-old kid and split for his friend's house. Being a complete douchebag, he left behind his fucking dog, which I had to rescue. So I packed as much of my stuff as I could into my Jeep and got the hell out of there.

I made it to Jay's friend's house when it hit me: whenever there's an evacuation order, looters come out. Even though I hated everything that weed stood for, I'd have to get my ass back into the fire zone to guard the pot we hadn't yet harvested, which was most of it. It was a shitty situation, but I'd spent all my savings getting out to BC and if we didn't sell that weed I'd come away from the whole project with nothing. Also, I still felt protective of that weed: I hadn't been able to grow it the way I wanted, but I had grown it.

I unloaded everything (including Kootenay and Jay's dog), then got back in my Jeep and drove into the fire.

I made it to the house. Everything was dark except for the flames all around me. I just sat in the front window, waiting. Sure enough, within the hour I saw vehicle headlights approaching.

Like I've said, I don't do guns and I don't do knives, so all I could do was grab a big rock and run out to meet the car, at which point I'd ask the driver what the fuck he was doing there. The car crept toward me, headlights shining straight in my eyes so I couldn't see what I was dealing with.

The car stopped.

The driver shut off the lights.

It was the fucking RCMP.

I WENT INTO dealing-with-police mode. "Good evening, officer," I said. "I know there's been an evacuation, but I'm the last one here, and I've cleared the property of people and animals and am about to leave myself."

"We'll be back in about twenty minutes," the cop told me. "And you better not be here."

"Don't worry," I said with a smile. "You see that Jeep right there? If *it's* not here, then *I'm* not here."

He left. I had twenty minutes.

I jumped into the Jeep and backed it up the narrow footpath to the greenhouse door, which meant taking out trees and shrubs and low-hanging branches. I ran into the baking-hot greenhouse and chopped down plant after plant and stuffed them in the back of the Jeep and the whole time I was choking and gagging since the air was so thick you could barely fucking breathe and all I could think was, The RCMP are going to be here any minute, any minute, any minute...

I put as much weed as I possibly could in the Jeep, stalks and leaves and nugs sticking out all over the place, then barrelled along the road out of the fire zone. And that's when I turned a corner and spotted a roadblock up ahead.

I couldn't stop: with all the weed in my vehicle, I'd get cultivation and trafficking and could do ten years in prison. They'd already spotted me so there was no way I could turn around. I couldn't even slow down, since all they'd see was a fucking wall of pot leaves speeding by. I had to go through it.

I knew they were there to stop people from driving *into* the fire, not from driving out, so I did the only thing I could: I rolled down my window and sped through the roadblock with a friendly wave, pretending like I was some guy who'd been slow to evacuate and was nervous about getting trapped.

I sailed right through, and did the forty-minute drive to Jay's friend's house in twenty.

OVER THE NEXT few days, we cleaned and cured and bagged the weed. We worked in silence. By that time we all fucking hated one another, and were depressed as hell since the pot, which hadn't been that good to begin with, had been fucking ruined by the fire. Later, Blue did manage to sell some of the campfire weed for chump change; my cut was a few thousand bucks, which wasn't even enough to get me and my Jeep back to Ontario.

He gave me the rest of the campfire weed and I moved onto the couch of a nearby friend named Stew, who we called DJ Indy since he was known locally for spinning at small clubs and parties. He put me in contact with a bunch of people to sell to. Slowly, I got rid of the pot. It took forever since it smelled so shitty, but after weeks and weeks of common street dealing, which I fucking *hated*, I finally scraped together enough money to get home.

GIVEN ALL THE trouble I'd had coming out to BC, there was no fucking way I was going to drive back to London. Instead, I packed up as much of my stuff into the Jeep as possible and put it on a train bound for Ontario. Then I bought a plane ticket home, which meant buying the biggest kennel I could find for Kootenay.

Even *it* fucked up on me.

At the airport they told me the kennel might be too big for the plane, so I sat at the window overlooking the plane being loaded. When they called my zone I asked if my dog made it on. They couldn't confirm, so I told them I wouldn't get on the plane until they could. Then one of the ground crew come up and spoke with the women at the gate, and I overheard the word *dog*. "Are you talking about my dog?" I asked them. Before they could answer I heard Kootenay's big nose sniffing away on the other side of the door.

It turned out the kennel had broken when the baggage handlers were trying to lift it onto the plane. Kootenay had escaped and ran around the tarmac at Vancouver International Airport. I guess he was running from plane to plane in the area, sniffing the luggage, trying to sniff me out. The pilots were calling into the control tower to report a black bear that had somehow gotten loose and was running amok.

They opened the door and there was Kootenay, wagging his tail, happy to see me. The baggage handlers took me back to the loading zone, where I helped them put Kootenay back in the kennel. This time they secured it with zip ties so the bottom wouldn't fall out.

I got on the plane, and flew home to a complete disaster.

THE LAST TIME I'd left The Organic Traveller in the hands of Bong Boy, he'd done a great job. This time, he'd hired five of his buddies to work in the store and some of them were complete deadbeats. One was a crack dealer. Another, a kid named Justin who called himself DJ Transit, started selling his own CDs from the store, offering Organic merchandise tax-free if the customer bought one of his albums. Soon after, Bong Boy started selling *everything* in the store tax-free, meaning the government didn't get its cut the whole time I was gone. Sure enough, within a month I got a letter from the Canada Revenue Agency informing me I was going to be audited.

A CRA auditor came in and I turned over my books. She complimented me on the clarity of the records, which I'd always done myself. What I didn't tell her was that I kept the books as simple as possible so that someone who was stoned out of their mind could still understand them. From them she could pretty much tell the day I left and the day I returned, just by figuring out when The Organic Traveller stopped and then restarted collecting sales tax. Later, the CRA sent me a bill for a bit over $36,000.

Meanwhile, I didn't have two pennies to rub together. This is how broke I was: while gone, I'd kept the house I rented on Oxford, but I'd turned off the gas, thinking I'd get it reactivated when (or if) I came back. Now, with the cold weather coming, I didn't even have enough money to get the heat turned back on: every night I'd sleep in my snowboarding gear to stay warm, or I'd sleep on a couch in the back of the store. Meanwhile, I still had to make the monthly rent and payroll on both The Organic Traveller and the Compassion Society.

Clearly, I needed to get some gardens going and make some money. To do *that*, however, I needed some start-up cash to buy clones and equipment, and cash was the one thing I definitely did not have.

So I went back to work at The Organic Traveller. This meant cutting Bong Boy's hours to next to nothing. He was pissed, and I was like, "Dude, if you'd paid more attention to your deadbeat friends, I wouldn't have to do this."

When Bong Boy's sketchy friends showed up, I told them I didn't want them in the fucking store. And they were all, like, What? Are you firing us? and I was like, "Man, I never hired you in the *first* place."

I should mention that he did hire a couple of truly good people. The first was Scott, who we called Blood Boy since he worked at the local blood bank. The other was Courtenay, who is known in the hip-hop world as DJ Everfresh. These two are still my friends and are truly stand-up guys.

Even though I had been working hard at turning The Organic Traveller around, I had run up debts to some of my suppliers that needed paying off before I could get new inventory, so I knew it'd be a while before the store started generating any real cash flow.

HERE'S WHERE A little positive karma helped me out.

As I've said, the AIDS Committee of London ran a needle exchange program called Counterpoint just around the corner from The Organic Traveller. A lot of junkies would go there, get their works, and then fix right outside my store, sometimes literally in the front doorway. Instead of getting mad at them—which wouldn't have helped—I got to know a lot of them, and I decided to start volunteering at the exchange, if only so I had some place to go after work that wasn't my freezing fucking house.

You might not expect a university town like London to have a thriving needle exchange, but London is really two cities. West of Adelaide you have the university, the insurance companies, the nice old Victorian homes. East of Adelaide is hardscrabble, working class, the place you settled when you were just trying to get by. It's starting to change a little, but London has traditionally been a city with a right side and a wrong side of the tracks.

As well, London is smack dab in the middle of a circle of small cities like Windsor, Sarnia, Kitchener, Waterloo, Guelph, and Woodstock. Through my work at the exchange, I found out that if an IV drug user got arrested enough times in those cities, the cops would just pick them up, drive them to London, and dump them on the streets. The cops just wanted the problem to move along, but knew that if they gave them enough money for a bus ticket they'd likely spend that money on dope.

So I was spending all my free time up at the needle exchange, handing out needles and alcohol swabs and collecting old dirty needles that clients brought in. Once, I accidentally poked myself with one, though I didn't freak out since I'm a firm believer that when my time comes my time is gonna *come*, no matter what I do about it. I put in so many hours up there that they eventually made me the interim coordinator, which was a lot to handle but I enjoyed the work and had a lot of success with it: we had a needle return rate of almost 80 percent, a figure I'm still proud of today.

When the director of the AIDS Committee of London, a woman named Shannon Dougherty, found out about my financial predicament, she did two things for me. First, she arranged a meeting with Union Gas, and claimed I was an individual who'd "been affected by HIV." Though this wasn't technically true, I did work with a lot of HIV clients at my compassion centre, and she figured this meant I deserved special consideration. Union Gas reconnected my heat on the understanding that I would pay back any reconnection charges, as well as the usual deposit, over time.

Then, Shannon arranged for the AIDS Committee to lend me $3,500.

THE FIRST THING I did was hire an accountant—a guy named Donny, who I use to this day—to structure a repayment plan with Revenue Canada. With the rest of the money, I bought enough equipment to start a small garden in my house on Oxford Street. When I say small I do mean small: my landlord at the time was really nosy and always coming around, so I kept it to two lights, tucked into a little room in the basement where no one but me would ever see it. I also started consulting on gardens again for cheap weed that I could use to supply the London Compassion Society, which my buddy Rob Newman had run effectively in my absence.

I was soon involved with indoor gardens all over the city, and as the first harvests came in I started to generate some badly needed cash flow. I also started brokering, even though it was never a business I enjoyed. But seeing as I was the man most closely associated with weed in the city, I was constantly getting opportunities, and because of my financial problems, I was in no position to turn them down.

One day I was working the counter at The Organic Traveller when this little bug-eyed kid came into the store. We started talking and he said he was from Toronto and had access to some good weed and hash, and would I be interested? I told him sure, and when he said he had some samples in his backpack I turned the sign on the door and we went into the back room.

Now normally, when someone says they have samples, they might have a gram or two to show you. *This* guy started pulling out full kilos from his backpack, all of it freeze-packed and stamped with Arabic writing. He was like, This kilo is this type of hash, and this kilo is *this* type of hash, and I get it straight from the source in Afghanistan so I can let you have it for a good price.

"How much?" I asked. The usual wholesale price for a kilo of Afghani hashish was about $5,000 to $6,000 at the time.

"Twenty-eight hundred."

I was like, "hell yeah, I'll take some." I'm pretty sure I even got him down to $2,500 a key. At these rates, I could sell to compassion clients at my usual reduced price and still generate enough profit to solve my financial problems. So I bought the lot.

The next month it was the same thing: he came into the store, a backpack full of freeze-packed kilos, asking if I'd like some more. I called him Davey Keys, and I still do business with him till this day, though now he's more into extracts and distillates.

After all these years, I *still* don't know who his contacts in Afghanistan were, or if they ever really existed. I've never even asked him: in the drug world, the less you know the better.

Around this time, I had another connection, a kid named John who we called 420 Spot. *He* was good for as much as sixty pounds of pot a week. Again, I had no idea where he got it all, and I didn't want to know: all I cared about was I was back on my fucking feet again.

16

BUSTED

THE LONDON COMPASSION SOCIETY was still offering holistic treatments and Steve's sometimes-nude yoga classes. My girlfriend at the time, Stephie, opened up a small massage school in the building. We also had a basement, where a few retail spaces had once operated. I figured why not get some more businesses in there.

I got an old skater buddy of mine named Tim—for some reason I called him Wally—to open up a store called Forest City Skate Shop. Then I helped another friend, a guy named John I'd lived with out on Twelve Mile Road, to open up an operation called The Friendly Farmer. Originally a section within The Organic Traveller, The Friendly Farmer sold grow equipment, and I figured with the right management it could grow into something big. I also helped open a glass blowing studio, which was run by a friend of mine named

Dane who went by the nickname Tubby, which was short for Tubby Two Shoes. (He actually wasn't tubby at all.) The basement was so massive I even had a little halfpipe ramp, which attracted people into the new skateboard shop.

All the businesses were profitable except Steve's yoga classes, which sort of fizzled out. In their place, I installed a massive "wheel garden." This was a new concept back in 2005: when growing indoors, one of your main challenges is duplicating the way the sun moves around the plants outdoors. There'd been all kinds of experiments with limited success, until someone came up with the idea of putting cannabis plants onto a sort of Ferris wheel, so that the plants moved around the lights. I'd heard that wheel gardens could double yields, and I was eager to test one.

Around this time, an apartment became available above the LCS space. As I've said, I had a really good relationship with Muky, the cannabis-friendly former building manager, who still worked for the building's owners. I'd been dealing with him for years and he was always willing to cut me a deal whenever possible. So when the apartment opened up, I talked to Muky instead of the new property manager, a woman named Sheila. (Or was it Shelley? I've blocked her name out of my memory since she ended up fucking me over so badly.)

I decided to rent it and install a garden. To look after the grow, I immediately thought of my cousin Kurt. (His grandmother and my grandmother were sisters, which actually made him my second cousin, but I always just called him my cousin.) Kurt was a couple of years younger than me, and had been a really successful pot dealer; when my various sources couldn't supply enough product for my

LSC clients, he'd often sold to me at wholesale prices. He was also into glass blowing, and for a time the two of us were partners in another glass blowing studio in London called Forest City Flameworks.

I ran the idea past him and he quickly agreed. So I told Muky I had a relative who needed a place; as I expected, Muky gave me a bit of break on the rent since I was already renting the whole first floor of the building. Kurt moved in, and the two of us installed a four-light garden.

A few months later, a second apartment opened up— again I talked directly to Muky, and this time rented the apartment for Albert, the LCS cleaning guy. I helped set up Albert and his partner Dave with a two-light garden.

The only problem was Sheila: I'd caught wind that she was complaining that when I rented directly from Muky she didn't get her commission for finding a tenant.

In 2006, a third apartment opened upstairs, and when I rented it as well she visited me at the store. "Pete," I remember her saying, "we gotta talk."

It was busy that day and I was in no mood. "What is it?"

"From now on, if you rent an apartment, you have to rent it from *me*."

All I could do was say sorry, but I'd been dealing with Muky directly for years, and that's just the way it was. She left pissed off. I can't remember if she actually threatened me, but I left feeling like there'd be trouble if I rented another apartment directly from Muky.

In early 2007, another apartment opened up, and again I rented it directly from Muky. When the first of the month rolled around, I took possession, installed a few lights, and plugged in another garden.

Three days later, I got a phone call from the police. It was early on a Friday morning.

"Is this Pete?"

"Uh, yeah..."

"I'm Constable So-and-So with the London Police Department. I'm at your garden."

"Which garden?" I asked, which wasn't the smartest question of all time, but fuck it.

"The one at 343 Richmond Street."

"Which *one* at 343 Richmond Street?"

"All of them," he said.

I immediately knew Sheila or Shelley or whatever the *fuck* her name was had phoned the cops. I said I'd be there as soon as I could. Sure enough, when I approached there were cops fucking *every*where. This was a windfall for them: not only had they found four apartment grows, they no doubt got my wheel garden as well. They'd likely never even *seen* a wheel garden before, which did look like something from outer space: sometimes the plants hung upside down to maximize exposure. You could see the excitement on the faces of the cops.

I parked where they couldn't see me, and left my cellphone in the car so they couldn't seize it. Then I walked on in. There was a cop standing right there. "Looks like you caught a marijuana grower," I said to him.

"We sure did. And who are you?"

"My name's Pete. You called me. I'm the grower."

"Just a minute," he said, and started mumbling into the walkie-talkie hanging off his shoulder.

Then a bunch more cops came around the corner. The funny thing was, they were all polite and respectful, not dickheads at all—they all knew me and had known what I'd been up to for, like, a decade.

"Pete," one of them said. "You know we gotta do this..."

I assumed the position against the wall. They searched me and found my PalmPilot, which held the numbers for every dealer, broker, and supplier I'd ever worked with. They confiscated it and I started freaking out. After they read me my rights, I asked if I could have my PalmPilot back to retrieve my lawyer's number. They handed it back to me; I put it back in my pocket and hoped to fuck they wouldn't remember and take it from me again.

At this point I noticed no one was paying me much attention, I guess since they all knew me and knew it was pointless for me to run. I think it helped that the cops *knew* I was anti-hard drugs, and only into marijuana and psilocybin. For example: most head shops sell little plastic bags used to package drugs. They come in two sizes: the larger ones hold a gram of pot, and the smaller ones are for pills and cocaine. I had made sure the cops knew The Organic Traveller only sold the bigger baggies. I also made a point of letting them know that Hi-Times, the other head shop in town, sold both. This way, if the cops ever picked up a hard drug dealer, they knew he wasn't getting his paraphernalia from me.

Or this: one day I found a small bag of cocaine in my shop that one of my customers must've dropped. I was good friends with Sergeant Price, the beat cop who walked my block, so I grabbed him the next time he walked by and told him someone had dropped a small bag of white powder in my store and I wanted to turn it in. He thanked me, and told me to hold on to it, saying he'd come by and pick it up. Another time I found a machete on the front stoop of The Organic Traveller. The blade was covered in red liquid, which was probably just red paint, but on the off chance it wasn't I told Price about the machete as well. Again, my attitude was we had to work together, the cops and I, so we might as well get along.

Meanwhile, the LCS was still full of fucking cops, and they were looking through everything while I stood there watching. The ones who knew me were all apologetic, saying, "Jeez, Pete, it was this complaint we got..."

"Don't worry," I kept telling them, "I get it. Just don't break any doors down, the landlord's done nothing wrong. I've got keys for everything, you just gotta ask, so don't bust into anything." In the end, they only broke down one door, which was pretty good given how many cops had showed up.

When they got to the bank vault where I kept my actual weed, I told them I morally objected to opening the vault, as it was full of medicine that sick people depended on. Then I opened it anyway, since along with the nice cops were a few bulging-neck-vein hard-ass dickheads who would've used battering rams to get in.

By the time the search was over, they'd found about five hundred plants in the four apartments and the yoga studio, as well as trays in my office containing nine hundred clones. (We were selling them to LCS members for five bucks a pop.) They also found about ten pounds of pot that I'd put aside for sale to LCS clients.

On top of that, they found about a pound of mushrooms, which were for my own personal use. I always bought in fairly large quantities because it's cheaper that way, and if kept in a refrigerator mushrooms can last quite a while without losing their potency.

While I was sitting in the back of the cop car, I remembered the small bag of cocaine in my office safe, the *same* fucking cocaine that Sergeant Price had forgot to come pick up, which pissed me off. So they didn't rip my office apart, I asked the officer in the car with me to contact the investigating officer regarding another item on the premises. They led me in to my office and I opened the safe under my desk and showed them the little baggy.

They arrested me and charged me with possession of a controlled substance, possession with intent to traffic, cultivation of marijuana, paraphernalia, and a few other bullshit charges I can't remember now. They also arrested Rob Newman since his name was on the lease for the centre. And they arrested Kurt and charged him with cultivation and possession.

They walked me to the car, and thank fuck they didn't put me in handcuffs—when I got in I discreetly pulled out my PalmPilot and, with a cop in the driver's seat, started erasing names. Every time I did the fucking thing would beep, so to mask the sound every few seconds I pretended to cough or sneeze or clear my throat.

We got to the station. They finally put me in handcuffs, saying it was just procedure and they had to do it. For my one telephone call, instead of calling Young, I dialled up one of the lawyers whose names were on a list tacked next to the phone; I figured since he'd be local he could get to court and bail me out come Monday morning. His name was Michael Barry, though his nickname, if you can fucking believe it, was Spike. Apparently, he used to be a champion wrestler back in college.

so.

Fingerprinting. Photographing. All that bullshit. When it came time for the interview, which was conducted by some cop I hadn't seen up to that point, I told him every gram of pot, every plant, and every clone, was mine. "Rob," I insisted, "was just an employee."

"And your cousin?"

"He just happened to live in the apartment with a garden, those plants were mine. I mean, the door to that room was locked."

"Yeah, but he had the *key* in his pocket."

"Okay, okay, I did give him a key, in case there was an emergency, but that garden was still all mine."

"What about the ounce of pot we found under his bed?"

"I... uh... took a nap there the other day and left my pot there."

"What about the half-smoked joint we found in the ashtray?"

"I smoked the other half."

"Pete," the guy said. "C'mon. Everybody knows you don't smoke pot."

"Well, I did that day."

He paused and looked at me. I could tell by his shit-eating grin he had something else. "And *what*," he said, "about the stuff we found in your cousin's refrigerator?"

"That pot was mine too."

"Pete. It wasn't pot."

"I meant mushrooms. Those mushrooms were mine too."

"It wasn't mushrooms, either. If you don't know *what* was in there, then it wasn't fucking yours."

It turned out Kurt had three LSD-soaked sugar cubes in his fridge, so in addition to his cultivation charge he was up against possession charges for both marijuana and LSD. I couldn't get them to let Kurt go.

I also couldn't get them to let Rob go. It was just like when Jordan and Sarah got arrested at Hemp Nation: he was working at the store, which meant he was "handling and participating" in the illegal activity being committed, blah blah fucking blah.

The interview lasted about forty-five minutes. When it was over, they took me to a single-person holding cell with a sleeping platform, a steel toilet, and cement walls.

After all my near misses, it was my first time ever behind bars.

AT THIS POINT, my biggest worry was my health. About a year before that, I was invited to play in a hockey tournament for musicians called The *Exclaim!* Cup—I remember some of the guys from the Barenaked Ladies, the Rheostatics, and Sloan were all there. I wasn't a musician but I did play drums in a drum circle, and I guess that was enough to get in. Our team was called The London Fog. During a game, I got hit really hard and was knocked out. When I came to I had a bad headache and blurred vision. I knew I had a bit of a concussion, but figured if I took it easy for a couple of days I'd start feeling better.

Five days later I felt even worse. The headache was still there, and my vision was now so fucked up I could barely read a street sign. I went to Emergency and they were, like, yeah, it sounds like a concussion, just keep doing what you're doing.

So I went home and got worse still: my head pounded, I was dizzy, and my vision was completely fucked up. I was also thirsty all the time—I couldn't drink enough water or Gatorade—and I was peeing four or five times a night. I was starting to get really worried, so I went back to Emergency and this time they said, "Hmmm, that might not be a concussion."

They tested my blood for sugar content and my reading was close to 70, or about ten times what it should've been. "Pete," one of the docs said, "you've got molasses for blood."

Diabetes, in other words. My father had come down with it two years earlier.

THAT FIRST NIGHT in jail, when the guards came around with dinner, all they had was white bread and bologna sandwiches. I told them I couldn't eat white bread, since I was a severe diabetic and it was pretty much *made* of sugar, and I couldn't eat the bologna since I was a vegetarian. The guard was like, "well, I'm sorry, that's all we got."

It's not safe for a diabetic to go hungry so I sat down thinking I was pretty much fucked. But a few minutes later, that same guard came back with bags of carrots and celery, which he'd gone across the street to buy. I thanked him, and crunched away.

I also told the guards I had to check my insulin levels every hour. This was sort of bullshit, since every four hours would've been fine, but sure enough they let me out every hour. I'd walk around, stretch my legs, check my blood in a little room reserved for medical cases, and then they'd put me back in the cell. At night I had to sleep on a slab of concrete and I woke up sore as shit. It was all boring as hell, but not so bad.

After a breakfast of more carrots and celery, they hand-cuffed me and put me in a paddy wagon. Rob and Kurt were both there, along with a couple of other recent arrestees. We were all pretty quiet as they took us to the joint.

17

HIGHLY FUCKING UNLIKELY

THE PRISON'S NAME was the Elgin-Middlesex Detention Centre, though everyone just called it Exeter Road. I took a look as I stepped out of the paddy. It was a low, brown, ugly brick building surrounded by high, razor-wire-topped fencing. They marched us all inside and took off our hand-cuffs and put us in a big holding cell full of prisoners.

For some reason they'd taken Kurt to another part of the jail, which left Rob and I sitting next to one another on a long, concrete bench. He told me he'd been charged and processed as well.

"Pete," he added. "I got one other thing to say."

"What's that?" I asked.

"I'm out of the dope business. You hear me?"

"I hear you," I said. To tell the truth I was as nervous as he was. At the time I had glass beads in my dreadlocks.

Rob, meanwhile, was flamboyantly gay. We stood out, and the one thing you *don't* want to do in prison is draw attention to yourself.

After an hour or so they took me to a range, leaving Rob in the holding cell. It was just like every prison movie you've ever seen, with one barred cell after another surrounding a day room. They gave me bedding and a towel, which I put in the two-person cell I was supposed to share with the two other guys who were already there.

I was just standing around in the common room wondering what I was supposed to do when three huge Native guys came up to me. The biggest one said, "Get the fuck in the shower and wash up."

I was like, "Dude, I'll wash up but I'm not taking a shower."

I went into the shower room and washed my hands and face. When I came back out, they were still standing there looking pissed off.

"Those're the fucking rules," one of them said. "You gotta take a shower." These guys looked like they wanted to kill me. I fucking *knew* this had nothing to do with whether I took a shower or not, and everything to do with who was the boss of whom.

Just then, someone yelled my name. I looked over, and saw some huge motherfucker grinning at me. He looked a little familiar, like maybe he was an Organic Traveller customer. He came over and explained to the guys that *this here* was Pete from The Organic Traveller, and that I was a good guy and nobody should fuck with me. This guy was obviously top dog on the range—the Native guys just shrugged their shoulders and walked off.

LATER THAT DAY, the Sunday edition of the *London Free Press* made it into the jail and my picture was on the front page, along with an article saying I'd gotten busted for mushrooms and LSD and cocaine and a whole shitload of marijuana.

Because of that article, I learned two things. The first is that cops exaggerate the value of drugs seized: they told the reporter the plants had a street value of $1.5 million. I'd have put it at maybe $40,000. They must've looked at all those clones and valued them as if they'd already grown into mature plants and been harvested, whereas I looked at them like what they were: seedlings I sold for five bucks a pop. Then again, they could've just upped the worth of the seized drugs to make their department look good, or to give the prosecutor a leg up at my trial, or maybe because people just naturally exaggerate their own accomplishments.

The second thing I learned that day is if you're in prison and your crime gets front-page coverage in the local paper, you get treated like fucking royalty. Everyone was coming up and saying, Hey, Organic Traveller, saw you in the paper man, one-point-five million! Jesus Christ, that's a ton of pot man, you think you could hook me up with some when I get out?

I'd only been at Exeter for a couple of hours, but I wanted to call my lawyer and figure out what was going on. I was in a short lineup for the phone when some huge dude tapped the shoulder of the guy in front of me and said, "This guy is next."

Then I went to watch television and it was just like in the movies, all these guys sitting on benches in front of the TV, and only the biggest guy on the range got to change the channel. I was watching something boring, not really paying any attention, when two of the Native guys from before sat one on either side of me. They still had those stony expressions, and I figured, Fuck, they're pissed at getting shown up earlier. I looked at one of them and then the other and *still* they hadn't said jack shit.

"So," one of them finally muttered, "you're Organic Traveller." He grinned from ear to ear. "Hey man, I bought my first pipe from you and this here's my cousin, fucking Joey, and he bought his first bong from you and since it was his birthday you packed a free bowl for him and listen, man, if you wanna change the channel you go right ahead..."

So that was jail. There were magazines and they did your laundry and the guards got me vegetarian food, and all in all, it wasn't that bad. On the outside, I'd been working all day every day, my phone was constantly going off, and I never had a moment to myself. Here, I finally got some time to do fucking *nothing*.

I remember turning to some guy and saying, "What do I gotta do to stay here?"

"See that guy?" he said while pointing to a guard. "Just go on up and slug him. You'll get all the time you want in here."

I SPENT THE night sleeping on a mat in my overcrowded cell. In the morning, we headed to court. Rob and Kurt were both in the wagon and we exchanged stories about our first night in jail. Somehow, one of the other inmates had a cigarette and he lit it halfway to the courthouse. This really pissed off the two cops up front, so they pulled into a parking lot and hauled us all out and searched us for contraband before piling us back into the wagon.

At the courthouse I met up with Spike, my lawyer. After waiting around for a while we went in front of the judge. It really sucked seeing my Pops and Kurt's mom sitting in the gallery; all I could think was that my family was going to hate me for getting my younger cousin caught up in this shit.

Bail was set for $50,000, which Spike paid on my behalf. Then, I was released.

When you get released on bail, the court sets a perimeter around the scene of your crime, and it's a breach of your bail conditions to enter that zone. In my case, that zone included my place of business, my accountant, my lawyer, my landlord, and my bank. It was pretty fucking severe. I learned that my case would be prosecuted by William Buchner, the same crown attorney who'd handled Chris Clay's case. We'd done everything we could think of to piss him off during that trial, so now it was payback time for him.

My movement restriction meant I had to meet with my various store managers in a parking lot just steps outside of my no-go zone, which is about as bad a way as you can imagine to run a business. I didn't even have Rob Newman to run the LCS for me anymore, and badly needed to find someone to take his place.

Then I heard from the Royal Bank: some tightass manager told me they no longer wanted to do business with me since I'd been arrested on an indictable offence. When he said I should come down and withdraw all my money, I had to tell him I couldn't do that since the branch was in the off-limits area defined by my bail conditions.

If that wasn't bad enough, my credit card then got cancelled. When I asked the credit card company what'd happened, they told me *I* was the one who'd cancelled the
card. This really pissed me off, so the next day I took a risk
and popped into my bank and emptied all my accounts.
The day after that, I called the credit card company, and
told them that they breached our contract by cancelling
my card and forging my signature to do so, and therefore
I wouldn't be paying the balance on the card. To this day, I
still haven't given them a dime.

WHEN THE LCS got raided, the cops also took about
$15,000 they'd found lying around. Now I didn't have
money to pay my rent on the Richmond Street spaces. I
asked Muky if I could defer some rent until I could generate
some more cash flow. I think he might've been willing to
do it, but he told me his boss was pissed that Farhi Holdings was mentioned in newspaper articles about the arrest,
so he couldn't.

The only thing I was able to keep at the Richmond
Street location was The Organic Traveller, because it was
still generating revenue: if there was one thing the publicity over my arrest *didn't* hurt, it was traffic to the store.
Everything else had to go—the compassion centre, the
therapy rooms, the holistic services, the yoga room, the
glass blowing studio, the hydroponic store, the halfpipe.

I moved the LCS into a much smaller space on Waterloo Street, which I shared with a tattoo artist named Joe.
It was a major step down from Richmond Street, but the
place had two advantages: it was outside my no-go zone,
and I could afford it.

The London Compassion Society was back, though in a bare-bones way. Since the new digs couldn't handle all the traffic, I went back to delivering cannabis door-to-door. At least this time I had a car to use for my deliveries.

I was again providing cannabis to medical users, which I admit was fucking risky. I'd just been caught with "$1.5 million" worth of pot, and had so many bail conditions I couldn't even remember them all. All I can say is, I might have been breaking the law, but I never believed I was doing anything *wrong*.

Also, I didn't believe the cops ever really wanted to bust me—they just felt obligated to raid the apartments that the "concerned citizen" had identified. How do I know this? During the raid, the cops found an electrical bill for the Oxford Street house. My little two-light grow there had grown to a much larger eight-light operation, so the bill was huge, like almost $7,000. The *obvious* next step would've been to search my house. But they never did.

So long as I wasn't too obvious about the tattoo parlour location, I felt like they'd look the other way. Remember: I was an inconvenience, a pain in the ass. After the Richmond Street arrest I'd done tons of media, and every journalist played up the Robin Hood angle, like I was just a little guy trying to sell weed to those who needed it to stay well. The cops never commented, which made them look like the evil Sheriff of Nottingham.

MEANWHILE, I REGISTERED for Legal Aid since I had no money to pay for a lawyer. Spike told me Legal Aid wouldn't pay him enough to fight my case if I chose to plead innocent. If I entered a guilty plea, however, he promised to get me the best plea bargain possible. So I agreed to plead guilty if, and only if, they'd agree to some terms.

The arrest happened on March 24, 2007. By December, Spike was in the office of the new federal crown attorney, some lawyer they'd shipped in to take over from that fuckwad Buchner. First, I wanted the Crown to drop all charges against Rob Newman and my cousin Kurt. Second, I wanted them to give me back the money they'd taken in the raid. Thirdly, I wouldn't do a day of jail time. If they promised all that, I said I'd plead guilty to possession of marijuana with intent to traffic, possession of psilocybin, and cultivation of marijuana.

The negotiations lasted a week. In the end, the Crown offered to give Rob a complete discharge. For Kurt, they dropped all charges related to the marijuana growing in his apartment, but gave him a conditional discharge for the LSD in his fridge: as long as he kept his nose clean for a year, he'd have no criminal record. (A couple months later, Kurt shipped a pound of pot to someone in Toronto and used his own credit card to pay for the courier. He got caught, and ended up doing weekends.)

As for me, I got six months of house arrest and, following that, eighteen months of curfew. I got on with business, which I have to say wasn't that hard under house arrest. Now, I could be in only two places: my house, where I grew pot, and my work, where I *sold* pot—the very crimes that'd landed me under house arrest in the first place.

I MADE SOME management changes. To run The Organic Traveller, I hired a kid called Matt who was an aspiring professional tattoo artist. We all called him Spanky, though, for very good reason.

One day when Matt was running the store, I found three things on the counter: a copy of *Playboy* magazine, a bottle of hand lotion, and a roll of paper towels. I was like, "Jesus fucking Christ, I don't give a fuck what you do in your off-time but you *cannot* be doing fucking *that* in the store!"

And he was like, "No, no, Pete, you got it all wrong…"

It seems he'd spent that morning getting a tattoo at a parlour across the street. A gorgeous young woman was in there getting a tattoo as well, and it turned out she was a local girl who'd got herself into the latest issue of *Playboy*. So Matt ran out and got a copy and had her sign it. Then he needed hand lotion to keep his new tattoo moist. And he grabbed some paper towels so that if he had to deal with a customer after putting on lotion, he could wipe it off.

A highly fucking unlikely story, in other words, but then he showed me the Playmate's signature across her belly. Still, you don't let something like that go, so I started calling him The Spankster, and then Spanky.

At the LCS, meanwhile, I put our former security guard, a tattooed biker named Marcel, in charge. He did a good job, having watched what Rob did for years. I also started gardens to replace the ones lost in the raid. Some of these were even legal, which is where my new girlfriend, Simone, came in.

I'd met her a year earlier at a yoga studio she'd opened with her partner, a friend of mine named Tony. We all went out for drinks one night, and while there was definitely a connection between us, she was with Tony so nothing happened. Cut to a year later: I was stopped at a gas station near her yoga studio when I bumped into her and discovered she'd split with Tony. We talked a bit about music, exchanged a few music links, and that night I asked her out. Within two months she was living with me at my house on Oxford Street.

At the time, Health Canada had started giving growing licences to individuals who met a certain illness criteria, so that sick people who benefitted from cannabis could grow their own weed and treat themselves. That person could also assign someone to grow *for* them, in case they were too infirm to do it themselves. The designated growers also had to meet certain criteria, a big one being that they'd never been convicted of a criminal offence. So that ruled me out. Simone met the criteria, so we got her "designated grower" status for a pair of very ill patients I knew. Using these licences, I rented a pair of warehouse spaces where we set up two sizeable gardens. All of this was completely legal.

Simone is the kind of person who just doesn't feel comfortable breaking the law. I've always been the opposite: if I want to do something, and I feel that it's morally just, then I really don't give a fuck what the law says.

This was a big break for me and the LCS. As I've mentioned, there were times when I was forced to buy weed on the open market to service all my compassion clients. With the warehouse gardens up and running, I had more than enough pot. It also meant my profit margin improved: at the time, the wholesale cost of pot was between $2,000 and $2,400 a pound. At the warehouse grows, it cost me about $600 a pound, meaning I could afford to lower my prices to LCS clients.

I've always been proud of having the lowest priced medicine in not only Canada, but all of North America. Back when I started, with little overhead, I was at $3.50 per gram. As overhead grew, so did my prices. Now that I'd cut that overhead, the prices at the centre dropped too, with strains as cheap as $2.50 a gram.

The rent on the tattoo parlour, meanwhile, was less than a third of what I'd been paying on Richmond Street, and pretty soon we were socking away money in order to return the LCS to a nicer location. Everything was looking up. I was in love and the centre was completely self-sustaining and I had my eye on a couple of key properties for the LCS, which I would've acted on quickly were it not for one delay.

In September of 2010, my fucking house was invaded.

HOME ALONE, TOO

I WAS AT HOME ALONE, watching television, when I heard the screen door open. and when I turned to look a fucking massive guy came charging in. He had to have been 6′6″, maybe 280 pounds.

"Police!" he yelled. "Get on the fucking ground!"

I held my hands up. "Wait a minute," I told him. "I'm a licensed grower and everything I'm doing here is legal," which was all horseshit but I had to say something.

"I don't give a shit, now get on the ground!"

So I lay down on my stomach and that's when I noticed another guy had followed him into the house.

"What the *fuck* is going on?" I yelled as the huge guy knelt on my back. When he fastened my hands behind my back with zip ties, and not handcuffs, I knew they definitely weren't the police. "I wanna see some badges."

"Shut the fuck up!" he yelled, and punched me hard in the back of the head. He grabbed my hair, he lifted my head up, and smashed it against the carpet.

"Where are the drugs, the money, and the guns?"

"Guns? Look around this place... I got *drums* on my walls."

He hit me again, *hard*, and I kept telling him I had a bad back, and I was a medical user, and he kept saying he wanted the drugs, the money, the guns. Each time I told him he was in the wrong house, and he'd punch me again. He was wearing those padded gloves that cage-fighters use but that made it hurt even fucking worse.

Eventually he let me sit up, and he started looking around. I managed to get my hands out of the zip ties and when he came close to me again I hit him with the closest thing to me, which was the TV remote, which did fuck all. He picked me up and slammed me on the floor and zip-tied my hands in front of me this time.

Then he really started beating the shit out of me. I might've even lost consciousness for a bit, but I came to when I heard Simone call out "hello?" from the back entrance of the house.

"Run!" I yelled. "Call the police, we're getting robbed!"

She took off and the big guy jumped up and went after her. So I jumped up and went after *him*, and that's when he picked up a dining room chair and broke it over the side of my face. Blood came out of my ears and nose, the was earth spinning, though I still had enough presence of mind to grab a knife. I cut away the zip ties and ran out the back door after the guy who was running after Simone.

I couldn't see either of the intruders, but I did see something even worse. After the raid on Richmond Street, I'd started keeping a lot of my harvested weed in bins in my front closet; now, the bins were in my backyard. Clearly they'd intended to take them, and would've if Simone hadn't happened to come home. I could hear her in the street, yelling that we were being robbed and assaulted and could someone call the police "please please *please!*"

I ran down the laneway yelling, "Did they come this way? Did they come this way?" A bunch of people had come out of their house or pulled over in cars and they all yelled no so I ran back up the laneway knowing it'd only be minutes before the fucking cops showed up.

Next door was a tiny bungalow I rented for Simone to use as a studio, so I ran back into the house and, feeling woozy as *fuck*, dragged all the bins of pot into there. Then I ran downstairs and locked the door on the room where I kept my eight-light grow, hoping to fuck the cops wouldn't ask me to open it. Then I locked the door to the basement and went back outside and sure enough, there were the cops, guns drawn, flashlights on, ordering me to the ground.

"No!" I screamed. "I'm the victim! I live here!"

They moved a little closer and that's when they saw my whole face was swollen and my legs were wobbly and I was bleeding. They had a look inside the house. When they got to the locked basement door I told them no one ever went down there and they said okay.

Did they know I had a garden down there? I dunno. It'd got so it was hard for me to know what the London cops did and did not know about what I was up to. All I know is if *I* was a cop, I would've wanted to have a look.

After that, they called an ambulance and I went to the hospital.

I WOKE UP the next morning with a fractured jaw, a bad concussion, and burns around my wrists from the ties. Some cops showed up and asked me if I knew who could've done this. I told them I didn't know, which was the truth, though after they left I started thinking about what might've happened.

On the other side of me was a rented house with this really sketchy motherfucker on the third floor who I was pretty sure was dealing hard drugs. Were they looking for him and broke into the wrong house? Or was it someone that read that bullshit in the papers about me being caught with $1.5 million worth of weed, and figured my house was worth breaking into?

I was still doing a bit of brokering, and I knew this guy in Toronto named Ron who I'd helped start a seed business about a decade ago. The week before the home invasion, Ron came to my house and I brokered a small deal, maybe ten pounds. As with the last couple of times I'd seen him, he was with a shady-as-fuck buddy of his he'd grown up with, a guy named Aaron. I knew him as a stain on the cannabis community: he never had a job, all of his income came from dealing drugs, and I'm pretty sure he sold drugs a whole lot stronger than cannabis. One look, and you could tell this guy was sketchy. His eyes literally shifted from side to side as he stood there saying fuck all. When doing any sort of drug transaction, you only involve people who absolutely *have* to be there. So I was like, "Ron, why the *fuck* is this kid with you again?" and he was like, "Pete, it's cool, he's a friend of mine, he's cool."

The very day I got out of the hospital, I was resting at home and who showed up but Ron and his douchebag friend Aaron. They wanted to know if I had any more weed to sell them.

I thought this was weird, since they were from Toronto and the shouldn't have to drive all the way to London to find weed. Also, Aaron was acting real nervous, even more so than usual, and I got the distinct fucking impression he had something to hide.

"No man," I told them. "I'm done with brokering. It isn't worth it."

Simone was there, and she was getting this really bad feeling about Aaron. I hadn't told her who he was, or how he was connected to me, but she's an empathic person and when they were gone she was, like, "that guy with Ron? There's something about him. I don't want him in my house again."

I took her advice. Ron started calling me every few days, and every time I saw his name appear on my phone I let it go to voice mail.

AFTER THE INVASION Simone was determined we should move. I was like, no *way* they're going to chase me out of my own house. I installed an alarm system and a surveillance camera, and made sure that the glass doors at the back of the house were always locked. Still, she was nervous as hell—wouldn't be alone in the house after dark, always had to know where I was, always looking over her shoulder when she walked out to her car. I started keeping pepper spray by the door and in the main rooms of the house, and I started carrying around a billiard ball. They're actually good weapons: if you throw it hard at someone it's going to crush whatever bone it hits.

I started having these wicked revenge dreams, the same two over and over. In one, I took the fucking cue ball and bounced it off my attacker's head and almost killed him, and then beat him with a piece of rebar I had stashed by the back door. In the second dream, I was driving up the long inclined driveway from the laneway to the parking lot behind our backyard. It was nighttime. When I crested the hill, my headlights lit up the back yard and there he was, the big guy, so I gunned the car and tried to fucking run him over.

Here's where it got really weird. One month to the *day* after the break-in, I was meeting with one of my gardeners one night and I forgot my cellphone in the car. When I went back for it, there were like a dozen missed calls from Simone, who was at home. I called her and she was fucking hysterical—she didn't know where I was, I wasn't answering my phone, she thought they'd broken in again and took me to some place where there was no cell reception.

I told her to relax, I was on my way home, but she was still fucking freaking out: she said she'd heard something or someone rustling around in the backyard. I told her it was her imagination but she was convinced there was someone out there, so she said she was leaving the house and would only come back when I let her know I was home.

"Alright," I said, and drove back to the house. Turning into my laneway I had to stop to wait for a young guy in a ball cap to walk by, probably a student I figured, since London is crawling with them. Then I drove up the laneway, and when I came over the top, my headlights hit the back-yard and it was just like in the dream: he was *there*, in my headlights, hands up to protect his eyes from the glare—the guy who'd fucking assaulted me.

I gunned it and chased him into the yard, but he hopped the fence into the neighbour's yard. I jumped out of the car and ran after him, which maybe wasn't the smartest thing to do but I wanted to fucking *murder* this guy. I was wearing Birkenstocks so I was a little slow, but I caught up enough to see there were two of them running away: the big guy and another guy, though not the same guy from the night of the break-in.

My common sense finally spoke up over all the adrena-line in my system. I ran back to my car and called 9-1-1 and told them I'd had a home invasion a month ago and now the same fucking guy had come *back*.

Then I drove down my laneway too fast; I bottomed out and the car made a loud clunking sound. So I stopped, and noticed that *same* student with the ball cap walking by again. Again, I didn't think anything of it, he was probably just coming back from wherever he was going the first time I'd spotted him. Since the car seemed to be running fine, I drove less than a block and that's when I saw the cops had come.

I got out and described the two guys. The cops went one way and I went another, racing up and down the side streets, talking to anyone I saw. Then I remembered that the last time they'd tried to rob me, they'd parked a get-away car behind the house. I raced back to the laneway, and there was that same fucking student walking by, only this time he had his hand up over his face like he didn't want me to recognize him. Sure enough, there was a car parked directly behind my yard, in the exact same spot they'd parked the first time.

I backed up into a driveway to turn around, but then steam started billowing out of the hood—it turned out I'd damaged the radiator when I'd bottomed out. I could see the ball cap guy walking up and down the street, acting all weird. By this point, I figured him for the driver and I couldn't understand why he didn't just get in the fucking car and drive away. I called 9-1-1 again and told them one of the guys was hanging around a suspicious vehicle parked beside my house.

"Don't worry," said the 9-1-1 operator. "Police have arrested the two men."

"No! There's a third guy!"

"Okay, okay, I'll try to get the police over there..."

"Look," I said. "I am *not* letting this guy get away, I've got a crowbar in my trunk and if those cops don't get here soon I'm going to kill the fucking guy."

"Do *not* do that," she said, and then she promised to have an officer call me. So I hung up.

A few minutes went by; still this kid was walking up and down the street, and still no call from the cops. So I said fuck it. I called my neighbour, who also happened to be the manager of The Organic Traveller. I asked him to look out his front window and tell me if he saw any cops. He did, so I instructed him to take his phone across the street and give it to an officer. I told the officer about the third guy, how he was parked on the street behind my house, and how I was going to beat him with a crowbar if they didn't show up *now*.

"Do not engage," the cop said. "Do you hear me? Do not engage. We'll be there as fast as we can." They showed up a minute or two later and picked the guy up.

After that, we were all standing around outside, and of course I was telling the police, "Don't worry, the burglars didn't go inside the house, no need to search, officers, no need at all." That's when the cops told me that before I'd called they'd received a call from a neighbour who had seen three men near my house putting on gloves and generally looking suspicious as shit, which was why they were already on their way when I'd called. They also told me they'd arrested a fourth guy I didn't even fucking know about.

LATER, I FOUND OUT something else that'd helped the cops get the guys. A good friend lived on the next street; he knew all about the home invasion, including the fact that the bad guys had parked right beside our house. On the night of the second attempt, they'd seen another car they didn't recognize, and cops all over the place, so they figured, Holy shit, it's happening again. They let the air out of the fucking tires, which was why the guy I thought was a student didn't just drive away.

My attacker got two years. One of the other guys had a knife on him, so he went down on a weapons charge. The other two got a slap on the wrist. Since they all pleaded guilty, no details came out about who they were, or why they'd targeted me.

I did learn one thing, though. They were all from Toronto. The only guy I did business with in Toronto was Ron. That's why today, I'm still convinced it was Ron's douchebag friend Aaron who orchestrated the whole thing.

A year later I ran into Ron at a cannabis conference in Toronto and of course he was with Aaron. I told Ron I knew his buddy sent those fuckers to get me and if he was still standing by him he was part of the problem and not the solution. Of course he denied it, but I just turned and walked away. I haven't answered a call from him since.

19

RED
DEVIL

AFTER THE SECOND INVASION, Simone flat-out refused to live at the house on Oxford, so we moved to a subdivision about twenty minutes northwest of London.

It was my second move that fall: shortly after the invasion, I found an awesome space for the LCS down at the opposite end of Wellington Street. It was a former accountant's office that had a huge loft on the second floor and skylights that let in lots of natural light, and it was on one of the major London bus routes, which was a real benefit to many of our clients. There was even parking. We put up a sign reading London Holistic Society, with the intention of using the front rooms for various therapies, and began renovations to replace some of the glass walls to make therapy rooms and add ramps for our clients in wheelchairs.

Around this time, I attended a medical marijuana conference in Toronto called Treating Yourself. We set up a booth at the tradeshow and covered it with photos of cannabis I'd taken for *High Times*. By the time the conference was over, we'd signed up about two hundred Toronto-based clients for a new mail-order program.

SHORTLY AFTER MOVING the LCS into the new Wellington address, my landlord called in the middle of the night to tell me there'd been a break-in and I needed to get down there in a hurry. I raced over and the place was crawling with cops. All I could think was if those cops were inside then I was going to jail.

I walked up to one of the police, a big older guy with a square jaw.

"I'm Pete," I told him, "the tenant."

"Looks like you got a broken window," he said. "But as far as we can tell the thieves didn't gain entrance."

"That's good."

"Still," he said. "I'd better do an internal, just to make sure nothing's been stolen."

"You really don't need to, I'm sure it's okay."

"Pete," he said. "I've got to go in."

I LET HIM IN. It was pitch-black inside. He followed me around, shining a flashlight on everything. My only hope was he didn't notice the menu of cannabis products tacked to the office wall, which he could've easily spotted by shining his light through the glass door. Instead, he pointed his flashlight up toward the loft, and said, "how 'bout up there?"

"I'll go check," I told him, knowing I had about ten pounds of pot up there, all divvied up and waiting to be distributed. I rushed up ahead of him and grabbed one of the batik wall hangings and threw it over the pot, which was on the floor, hoping that it'd look like a carpet. One second later, the cop stepped up and shined his flashlight into the room.

The place *reeked* of pot. They *knew* they were in the offices of an underground compassion centre. They also would've known I was still under house arrest for a fairly major drug conviction. But what did he do? He peeked in for a second, and said, "okay, it looks like the premises are secure, have yourself a good night."

Five minutes later, they were all gone, and I was on the phone trying to get the broken window replaced.

SOON AFTER, I discovered a problem with the Wellington location. Right across the street from us was a Montessori school. There was a second Montessori location right behind us. Each day, parades of children walked by our front door. I don't know how I didn't notice it earlier. I hadn't smoked pot for five years by now, I should've fucking noticed not one but two elementary schools right beside the store.

One day, I was sitting in my office, when our receptionist called and told me the cops were at the front. So I went out and there were two uniformed police officers and this little five-foot-fuck-all chick with a clipboard, who introduced herself as the local bylaw officer.

The room was full of LCS clients buying weed. "Can we step outside?" I asked. Once we did, she explained I wasn't zoned for offering holistic medical treatments.

"But there's a massage clinic right around the corner."

"Yes but these two houses"—she pointed at my location and the one next door—"are only zoned for accounting or real estate." It sounded like bullshit: since when did you have a special zone for just two addresses, and two specific professions?

She then described an insane six-month process to apply for the proper zoning, which would mean I'd have to shut down for a half a year with no guarantee I'd get the right zoning in the end.

"We done here?" I asked.

"We are," she said.

"Then I think these guys want to chat with me," I said while motioning at the cops.

"Have a good day," said the bylaw officer. When she was gone I turned to the cops and asked them what all this was about.

"Lookit," one of them said. "We know what you're doing here. We've been watching who comes in and out of this place. We know you aren't selling to children but still, we've been getting complaints from parents, you follow?"

I said I understood they had a job to do, but so did I. At the end of our twenty-minute conversation, they gave me a piece of advice: "Here's what you do: you make the city happy, and we'll make you happy."

I stood looking at them. A client on a Harley pulled up, walked in, got his pot, and walked back out. The cops didn't blink.

"So I move?"

"Yeah," the cop said. "You move."

WE FOUND A potential new place right away, thanks to the help of a real estate buddy. Thankfully, my house arrest was over, meaning I could actually go and see it.

It wasn't much to look at from the outside, just an indiscrete little house in the northwest corner of downtown. Inside, the place was in rough shape. The previous tenant had run some sort of spa. Apparently he was a good guy who always paid his rent, but then, in the middle of the night, the guy just fucking disappeared. While the house sat empty, some people broke in and spent an entire weekend pulling out all the electrical wiring, the plumbing, and the fucking water meter. The landlord figured it must've been desperate junkies—who else would work that hard for eighty dollars' worth of copper?

Still, there were things I liked about the location. It was a gorgeous spot, away from the busyness of downtown, with a long beautiful lawn extending down to the Thames River that runs through the heart of the city. It had parking and was on a bus route. There was already a wheelchair ramp leading to the side door. Plus, the place was big, with enough space for a waiting room, kitchen, reception area, product room, and a huge room at the back where, in time, I figured I could start up my safe-inhalation site.

The deal-sealer was the landlord: when I told him what I'd be doing with the property, he was totally cool. "Look Pete," he said, "my last tenant ran away in the middle of the night. As long as you pay your rent on time, and treat the place respectfully, I couldn't give a *fuck* what you do in here." So I took it.

The landlord got to work fixing the place up, including the plumbing, which had somehow backed up while the house sat empty. He soon learned why: he found about 150 condoms in the sewer line. Right then and there, he knew what'd probably happened. During the day, the guy had run a legitimate spa. But at night, it was a rub 'n' tug. In London, anything to do with sex work was run by bikers, and they're known for not taking kindly to other people stepping on their turf. Our guess was they'd found out about this guy's after-hours operation and paid him a little visit.

AS THE WORK proceeded, Simone and I got married. For a date, we chose December 21, 2012, which is otherwise known as the end of days predicted by the old Mayan calendar. I figured it'd be a good day to get married: if the universe really *did* end, I wouldn't have to pay all my wedding bills.

We invited 120 people to the open-bar reception, held on the grounds of the Elsie Perrin Williams Estate, a heritage building used for public events. I wore my new hemp suit. Simone and I were really into making wine at the time, and it was good enough that we served it at the wedding. A year later, we went ruin hopping in Mexico and called it a honeymoon.

THE LCS MOVED into the new location in January of 2013. No sign, completely discreet, and, as always, we *insisted* on a doctor's prescription before we served anybody.

Our client base grew. We installed video cameras and a buzzer system, and opened three days a week. We sold by appointment only, so we could have the orders ready and customers were in and out in less than five minutes. For clients who didn't have transportation, or had illnesses that affected their movement, we offered home delivery (as well as mail order for clients living elsewhere). This made our business more efficient, and meant we didn't have a lot of people hanging around waiting for their orders. It also added to the confidential air of the London Compassion Society.

Our competitors went a different route. A few years after we set up shop along the river, some outsiders decided to get in on the game, and of course they put up huge fucking neon signs, with names like Tasty Buds and Chronic Hub.

While they claimed to sell only to medical users, you just fucking *knew* they weren't too choosy when it came to doctor's prescriptions. One of them would take customers into the back and have them Skype with some crooked physician. This doctor—and who knew if he even *was* an MD—would email the prescription and the customer would get an extra charge for the consultation.

It was quite a fucking racket. My whole life, I'd fought against the perception that "compassion centres" were a dressed-up type of street dealing. And now, these businesses were moving in that really *were* one small step above common dealers. The cops must've thought so too. They ended up raiding every "dispensary" in London, with one exception: they didn't touch the LCS.

BUSINESS KEPT GROWING: eight hundred clients, a thousand clients, twelve hundred clients. To meet the demand, I ramped up production at the warehouses, rented more apartments to house grow-ops, and sponsored more gardens tended to by others.

If one of my growers showed some talent with a particular strain, I'd let them focus on that strain. For example, there was a guy we called Hootie—since he looked like the guy from Hootie & the Blowfish—who concentrated on one of our own strains called Lemon Skunk. Another guy we called The Italian grew our Northern Lights. Yoda grew our Hawaiian Snow, though he used to be known for a strain called Widow 98. I had another guy we called Manatees who, on top of working in the store, grew a strain called Strawberry Devil.

And then there was Jay, a cocky kid who had a really fucking awful disease where there was too much metal in his blood. When I met him—this was a few years ago—his condition had made him weak as shit and had pretty much rendered him a shut-in.

He was growing some mediocre strains in a two-light basement grow. So I set him up with a fucking potent indica we called Red Devil. It was so strong that a lot of our clients didn't like it. I did, however, know of a group who probably *would* like it: the judges of the Toronto Cannabis Cup. I figured that success at the Cannabis Cup might help his recovery.

It was held on a boat that cruised around Toronto Harbour, a pretty common practice for cannabis cups to help avoid interruptions. (Although more than one cup has ended with police boats circling, pounds of pot floating in the water, and stoned entrants swimming for shore.)

As everyone knows, marijuana is a heady drug, with the user's perception of the drug's effects almost as important as the drug itself. As a grower, you can try to influence this perception to your advantage, like I had tried to do in Amsterdam when I'd spent all of my time flirting with the female judges.

I did the same with Jay's weed. Since Jay couldn't talk to people, I was the one who went around telling people how fucking strong it was, like "This shit's the bomb, man, don't even *think* of driving after you've smoked some, and just between you and me you might want to have one straight person around in case things get a little hairy, you know what I mean?" On and on I went, making it sound like it was the most powerful pot ever grown. At the end of the day, Red Devil won best in show. After that I noticed Jay was more apt to get out of his apartment, and more optimistic about his condition.

I didn't attend the following year. I did, however, send in two strains that I'd grown, an indica called Jilly Bean and a sativa I can't remember the name of. Both took gold, even without me being there to prime the judges.

And then, in 2015, along came Indiva.

MASTER
GROWER

INDIVA IS AN "Authorized Licensed Producer of Cannabis for Medical Purposes," or a Licensed Producer for short. This means that the Canadian government has granted it the legal right to both grow cannabis and produce cannabis-related products, and then sell them to individuals with a medical certificate from Health Canada—and, as of October 17, 2018, to anyone at all. It operates out of a state-of-the-art, high-security cannabis production facility on the outskirts of London, Ontario.

I'm the master grower here, though it's a term I don't like since I don't consider myself a "master" when it comes to growing pot: I might know more than some people, but I also know people who know a whole lot more than me. My old girlfriend Artemis, for example, is running medical marijuana grows out in California, and I just know there are things she could teach me. More importantly, cannabis is a living being: it evolves every day, and even the most novice grower can unlock new mysteries regarding its inner life. When it comes to growing pot, no one's a master.

Today, Indiva is where I mostly spend my time, wandering through a massive plant filled with cannabis, worrying about things like the supply-storage water feed system, the automated fertilizer system, the Dosatron nutrient pumping system, the spectrum-corrected HID lighting systems, etcetera, etcetera...

To enter the plant, you're first buzzed through a sixteen-foot-tall sliding chain-link fence with razor wire and weight sensors. I once threw a shovelful of snow at it and an alarm went off—a fucking pain in the ass, since we have to make a report for every "security breach." Then you're buzzed through the front entrance, where you sign in and get buzzed through another door, your every movement captured on security cameras, and you're still nowhere near the fucking plants.

To do that, you have to take off your clothes, put on a sterile gown and mask, and have an ionizing foot bath, at which point you pass through a few more locked doors. Only then do you start reaching the heart of a licensed cannabis production facility: the mother room, the veg room, the cloning room, the flower room, the trim room, the drying room, the vault.

Every door along the way only opens upon entering a code. There are intercoms and buzzers and cameras everywhere. The walls are made from ten-inch reinforced concrete. I'm told that the plant was built according to "level 9 security protocol," which basically means it would take a military tank to get inside. And even *it* would have some trouble.

Every seed, every cutting, every brown and fallen leaf has to be counted, weighed, bagged and reported to the government. This is to prevent employee theft. Health Canada representatives have the right to surprise inspect the facility whenever they please in order to make sure we aren't fucking up in any way.

To be alone with the cannabis, you have to have a level of security clearance called Responsible Person in Charge, or RPIC. I can't qualify for RPIC status since I have a criminal record. So if I ever want to be anywhere near my plants, I have to bring someone with RPIC status with me. At Indiva, our RPIC is a PhD in chemistry named Danny. I have to say he's pretty patient about following me around all day.

MY NEW GIG is all thanks to Davey Keys, the guy with the connection in Afghanistan. Shortly after the LCS moved into its final location, Davey told me he knew of a couple of guys in London who were applying to become a Licensed Producer. I got on board by investing about $40,000.

Two other partners, both based in Ottawa, got involved shortly after. One was a business lawyer named Koby Smutylo who, like me, did yoga and practiced vegetarianism. The second was a guy named Niel Marotta who used to run an investment fund in Boston. Both of them were the type of guys with access to larger investors, and both had been looking to get in on the ground floor of legal marijuana production in Canada.

Due to some personality conflicts, Koby and Niel bought out the original players, at which point they asked me to stay involved as a partner and master grower for the company, which they were now calling Indiva—a mash-up of the words indica and sativa. I asked them what they'd give me. They came back with a contract offering me a six-figure salary and a nearly 20 percent stake in the company. I showed it to my lawyer, who disliked some of the finer points. There was some dickering, but in the end I signed off.

At this point, Koby and Niel went off and raised about $40 million. (As I write this, that figure has climbed to over $60 million.) Then they leased an entire industrial mall out by the highway. Construction of the facility started in February of 2016. Since then, a bunch of staff have been hired, including my old friend Sarah Delaney, who was arrested at Hemp Nation all those years ago and then worked as the receptionist at the LSC, at least until *it* got raided. I'm amazed she agreed to work with me again, but she's head of client care at Indiva, and I see her almost every day. I also hired an old college buddy named Andrew Zwicker—or Zwick, as we call him—to work in production. I figured he was qualified, since he's been growing cannabis up near his home town of Orillia for years.

We finally received our licence in July of 2017. We started growing by September. There was a bit of a problem finding mother plants—according to the licence they had to come from a Health Canada-accredited source, which turned out to be tricky. Still, in early 2018 we harvested our first crop, an indica called Day Break Kush that passed a rigorous Health Canada inspection.

The Canadian government under Justin Trudeau has just passed Bill C-45, "An Act respecting cannabis and to amend the Controlled Drugs and Substances Act, the Criminal Code and other Acts"—as of October 2018, recreational use of marijuana is completely fucking *legal*. As a result, the various private and government marijuana dealers will be obligated to buy from licensed producers such as Indiva.

Which brings me to now. We're upping production at Indiva as the plant expands into its full space. As founding director of the London Compassion Society, I still pop in from time to time, and watch my employees distribute illicit pot to about fifteen hundred clients. We have twenty-four varieties of indoor pot and eight varieties of outdoor pot. Of those thirty-two varieties, all are grown either by myself, in various undisclosed locations around London, or in gardens that I helped start, and as a result sell exclusively to the centre. We also have edibles, infused honey, capsules, oils, tinctures, topicals, and extracts.

So there you have it. I work on both sides of the law, now. The LCS is illegal, Indiva is legal. I also build houses on the side; I still believe it's immoral to make your whole living from pot, even if you can easily do so. With all this going on, my head still spins with details, and I find myself waking up at four in the morning, unable to switch my brain off, so I get up and answer emails.

I have two dogs, a couple of customized motorcycles, and a fully restored, lime green 1972 Karmann Ghia I keep on a lift in my garage. I also have a 1978 Volkswagen Westfalia; last summer, Simone and I put fourteen thousand kilometres on it, driving to and from music festivals in the

US. We also keep an old motor home in Reno, Nevada, that we use when we go to Burning Man.

I travel a lot. As the public face for Indiva—they have T-shirts with my picture on them—I do a lot of speaking at pot-related conferences, and I do things like ring the bell at the opening of the Toronto Stock Exchange. I also go to hot places with Simone a lot: Bali, Thailand, India. On my last trip to Mexico—we went to see a jam band called Widespread Panic play at the Hard Rock Hotel in Los Cabos—my fucking diabetes went haywire on the plane ride home, and that landed me in hospital for a week.

So you never know what can happen. The pot game is a crazy one, and lately I've been thinking maybe I've put in my time. I'm in the back half of my forties now. Maybe fifty would be a good time to call it. If I do retire, Simone and I will probably move someplace south, and then see the world via house trades. Maybe I'll build a cottage up in Northern Ontario, and spend the summer months here so we don't get homesick. I'll also get rid of my phones, so nobody can reach me. That'd be nice.

Either way, when I'm finally done and I've grown my last plant and sold my last gram, I'm hoping I look back on all I've done and get the big picture.

This can be hard. You go about your day, and it's one problem after another, and you're always thinking about what's fucking up and not about what's going right. It's easy to get stuck on the forest and miss the fucking trees. But on the day I finally pack it in, I'm hoping I remember one thing clearly: when I was fifteen, my friends and I were always like, Man wouldn't you *love* to make a living out of selling or growing pot? Wouldn't you love to do this *full-time*? Somehow, I did it. I might've had some experiences I didn't fucking *want* to have, but I did it.

I helped a lot of people and I met a lot of interesting people and I went to a lot of interesting places and I saw the inside of jail cells and I had my jaw broke and I towed U-Hauls full of drugs and I kept hundreds of pounds of pot in warehouse freezers and there were times I couldn't afford to turn on the heat and other times I had to buy a cash counter to keep track of all the money that was coming in. Once, I manned a pot-conference booth for a Vancouver-based bed and breakfast called Sativa Sisters; to attract attention they put me in a bright pink G-string.

Yet today, I'm the guy who walks around a huge plant all day, working under artificial lights, dealing with suppliers on the phone, worrying about production schedules, complying with government regulations, making sure everything gets done on time, and I can't help but think: Is this me? Is this really me?

It doesn't matter, not really, not when time doesn't mean a whole lot in the big scheme of things. When you look at the whole of it, at the mandala of it, at the entire yin-yang of it, all you can think is, Dude, you did this, you fucking did this, you did.